中国洛阳出土唐三彩全集

Collected Works on Tang Tricolor Unearthed in Luoyang, China

(上)

周立　高虎　编

大象出版社

图书在版编目(CIP)数据

中国洛阳出土唐三彩全集/周立，高虎编.—郑州：大象出版社，2007.4
ISBN 978-7-5347-4414-3

Ⅰ.中…　Ⅱ.①周…②高…Ⅲ.唐三彩－图集　Ⅳ.K876.32

中国版本图书馆CIP数据核字（2007）第027076号

选题策划　耿相新
责任编辑　郑强胜
特约编辑　王　月
整体设计　文　语

出　　版　大象出版社
　　　　　(郑州市经七路25号　邮政编码450002)
网　　址　www.daxiang.cn
发　　行　河南省新华书店
制　　版　郑州**书犁图文**设计有限公司
印　　刷　郑州新海岸电脑彩色制印有限公司
开　　本　889×1194　1/16
版　　次　2007年4月第1版
印　　次　2007年4月第1次印刷
印　　张　40
字　　数　800千字
ISBN 978-7-5347-4414-3
定　　价　680.00元

序 言

欣闻周立、高虎同志主编并拍摄的《中国洛阳出土唐三彩全集》即将出版发行，很为他们高兴。周立、高虎同志是长期工作在田野考古发掘一线的文物摄影专业干部，具有丰富的文物摄影经验。他们用高超的摄影技艺，赋予了洛阳唐三彩新的生命活力，展现给读者的是栩栩如生的唐代众生相，带给大家的是赏心悦目的美好享受。希望他们在今后的工作中再接再励，为洛阳的文物工作做出新的贡献。

《中国洛阳出土唐三彩全集》是继文物出版社1980年出版《洛阳唐三彩》和河南美术出版社1985年出版《洛阳唐三彩》之后又一部有关洛阳唐三彩的大型图集。在不到30年的时间里，先后就出版了三部唐三彩图集，这三部图集收录的唐三彩，并非重复使用，每部都有上一部中未收录的新品种、新形象。由此可见洛阳唐三彩资源之丰厚。

从上述《洛阳唐三彩》问世至今，才过去20多个春秋，在这短短20余年的时间，洛阳在配合基本建设中，发掘了大批唐代墓葬，在这些墓葬中出土了不少珍贵的历史文物，而唐三彩就是这些珍贵文物中的一类，其数量之多可达上千件，品类之新也是前所未见的。为了进一步弘扬洛阳的唐三彩文化，让洛阳和全国人民了解洛阳在唐代考古工作中取得的丰硕成果，有必要再出版一部唐三彩的大型图册，也就是即将问世的《中国洛阳出土唐三彩全集》，作为《洛阳唐三彩》的续篇。

通过《中国洛阳出土唐三彩全集》的出版，一定会唤起洛阳人民对洛阳的古墓葬、古遗址、古文物的保护意识，自觉地保护洛阳的古墓葬、古遗址、古文物不受破坏，不遭盗掘，不被走私贩卖。

通过《中国洛阳出土唐三彩全集》的出版，可以让全国人民、全国的文物考古界同仁，了解洛阳唐三彩文化底蕴之厚。要了解唐三彩吗？只有到洛阳、西安。要研究唐三彩吗？也只有到洛阳、西安。除这两地之外，没有更合适的地方，因为这两地是唐三彩的故乡，是唐三彩的发掘地，是丝绸之路的起点。

唐三彩虽然只是一件件的马、骆驼、各种人物、各类器皿，但这些俑类，这些器皿，却蕴含了丰富多彩的文化内容，它们不仅反映了当时高超的雕塑、绘画、陶瓷工艺水平，同时反映了当时的民族风尚，社会的繁荣昌盛，东西文化交流和东西商贸的盛况。一句话，它们是盛唐盛世的一个缩影，也是洛阳盛唐时期的缩影。鉴于此，我认为《中国洛阳出土唐三彩全集》的出版，一定会受到雕塑界、美术界、陶瓷界、收藏家、鉴赏家们的欢迎和喜爱，一定会得到研究唐史，研究唐代丝绸之路的专家、学者们的重视。

通过出版这一大型图集，我希望洛阳的文物考古者将洛阳文物考古工作中的丰硕成果以及科研领域中所取得的丰硕成果，更多、更快、更好地奉献给社会和大众，这是我们文物考古工作者的责任和光荣使命，大家应该义不容辞地承担起这个任务，积极地完成这一光荣使命，同时也希望洛阳的文物考古工作者在新时代、新机遇面前更加努力地提高自身的业务水平、科研水平和工作能力，用科学发展观的思想来面对时代的挑战、新机遇的挑战，为宣传洛阳、塑造洛阳崭新的形象，弘扬洛阳博大精深的古老文化，谱写新的篇章。

郭引强

2006年11月8日于洛阳文博大厦

PREFACE

It is a pleasure learning the publication of *Collected Works on Tang Tricolor Unearthed in Luoyang, China* edited and photographed by Zhou Li and Gao Hu , who have been engaged in the field of archaeology for a long time as professional photographers. With abundant experience and superb photographic skills, they make *Tang Tricolor* more vigorous and vivid, presenting various acts of the people in the the Tang Dynasty. I believe they will redouble their efforts and make new contributions to the historical relic work in Luoyang.

Following *Tang Tricolor in Luoyang* published by the Cultural Relics Press in 1980 and by Henan Fine Arts Pub-lishing House in 1985, *Collected Works on Tang Tricolor Unearthed in Luoyang, China* was another grand picture collection. During less than 30 years, there have been three picture collections of Tang Tricolor published successively, each of which adds new varieties and images. Thus it is obvious that Luoyang is rich in the resources of Tang Tricolor.

It has been just more than 20 years since the first picture collection on Tang Tricolor was published. During these years large quantities of the graves of the Tang Dynasty have been discovered in the course of constructing Luoyang, and many precious historical relics have been excavated such as Tang Tricolor, the number of which can approach 1000 with unprecedented varieties .In order to further carry forward the cultures of Tang Tricolor in Luoyang and make the achievements in archaeology of the Tang Dynasty known to the people all over the world ,we publish another large-scale picture collection of Tang Tricolor named *Collected Works on Tang Tricolor Unearthed in Luoyang, China* which will be taken as the continuation of *Tang Tricolor in Luoyang*.

The publication of *Collected Works on Tang Tricolor Unearthed in Luoyang*, *China* will arouse Luoyang people's consciousness of protecting the ancient tombs, sites and antiques and keeping them from being destroyed, stolen and smuggled.

In addition, all the people and all the peers in the archaeological field of historical relics will learn about the detailed culture of Tang Tricolor. If you want to know and study Tang Tricolor, Luoyang and Xi' an are the best choices, as they were the excavation sites of Tang Tricolor and the starting point of the Silk Road.

Tang Tricolor products refer to the potteries of horses, camels, various terra-cotta figures and household utensils with rich and colorful cultures, They not only reflected the skilled sculpting, painting, and ceramic handicrafts of that time, but also revealed the contemporary customs, the social prosperity and the grand occasions of the cultural exchanges and trades between the east and the west. In short, they were epitomes of the flourishing Tang Dynasty as well as the booming Luoyang in the Tang Dynasty. In view of this, I believe the publication of *Collected Works on Tang Tricolor Unearthed in Luoyang, China* is sure to be popular with the sculpture circle, the art circle, the ceramic circle, collectors and appreciators, and it will be valued by the experts and scholars studying the history and the Silk Road of the Tang Dynasty.

Through the publication of the large picture collection, I hope the workers of historical relics can achieve more archaeological fruits in scientific research and contribute more to the society and the masses, and the sooner the better. This is our responsibility and glorious mission. We should undertake the duty unshakably to fulfill it. And at the same time, I also hope the archaeological workers in Luoyang can make more efforts to improve their own professional skills, scientific research standard and working abilities, so that they can meet the challenges of the times to take new opportunities with the thought of scientific development, shape and publicize the brand-new image of Luoyang, and carry forward its extensive and profound ancient cultures.

written by Guo Yinqiang

Wenbo Mansions in Luoyang on November 8, 2006

前 言

洛阳是发现唐三彩最早的地方，20世纪20年代末陇海铁路修到洛阳城北的邙山脚下，发现了大量的唐墓，出土为数可观的随葬品，包括唐三彩，从此埋在地下一千多年的艺术瑰宝——唐三彩得以重见天日。这种未见于文献记载的多彩陶器在古都洛阳的惊现，人们称之为“唐三彩”。一时消息传开，轰动了全国，惊动了世界的文物考古界、古玩界、收藏界，风靡各国的艺术界人士，顿时纷纷云集北京、洛阳，竞相搜求，高价收购。被人们早已遗忘的历史古都，因此而唤起了人们的注意和重视。洛阳以文物之美、文物之丰富而闻名，这种闻名，当时在全国各地是没有的。金村大墓的又一次轰动，更加确定了洛阳在文物界、艺术界、古玩界、收藏界的地位。

洛阳不仅是发现唐三彩最早的地方，也是生产唐三彩的故乡，一方面是洛阳出土的唐三彩数量多，如此众多的形形色色的唐三彩，全部为外地运来，这是不可想象的，因为它属于易毁易碎的陶瓷器，稍有不慎就会成为废品。可见，洛阳出土的唐三彩，主要是就地取材、就地烧造、就地销售。当然也不排除有西安产品。我们说洛阳的唐三彩主要为洛阳自己烧造的，这是有依据的。唐王朝建立以后，洛阳与长安一样，政治稳定，经济发达,商业贸易兴盛，这一切为唐三彩的生产提供了保障和市场，同时洛阳陶器手工业历史悠久，技术成熟，就瓷器而言，洛阳在唐以前两千余年就可烧造成熟的青瓷，而低温釉陶在汉代已出现,加之洛阳原料丰富，这一切都说明洛阳完全具备了自己烧制唐三彩的条件，更重要的是烧制唐三彩的窑址在唐代洛阳辖区内的巩县已有发现，地址就在今巩义境内的大小黄冶村。而窑址中残存的三彩片种类、胎片、釉色等与洛阳出土的唐三彩基本上属同类产品，可见洛阳的唐三彩是巩义烧制的，是否在洛阳周围还有唐三彩窑址呢?目前尚未发现，可以肯定地说应该是有的，因为洛阳所需唐三彩只靠巩义供应是满足不了需求的。洛阳是烧制唐三彩的中心，但不是唯一的中心，西安也是其中心。洛阳与西安都是唐三彩的故乡，这两个故乡应该是同时出现的，所谓同时，不是同一年,而是同一个时期。唐三彩不仅在洛阳、西安有发现，在全国的南方、北方、西北、西南、东北的不少地区都有出土，这些地区的唐三彩风格都不尽相同，也各有特色，而与洛阳、西安的唐三彩也存在一定差异，可见这些地区的唐三彩无疑也是就地取材，利用自己的技术烧造的。当然他们烧造的唐三彩摆脱不了洛阳和西安的影响。洛阳和西安是生产唐三彩最早、最多的地方，是唐三彩生产的源头。

唐三彩是一种低温铅釉陶器。所谓唐三彩并非只有三种彩釉,而是以黄、绿、白或黄、绿、赭为主。还有深绿、浅绿、翠绿、黑、蓝、褐等多种色彩，可见唐三彩实际上是多彩釉陶的总称。 唐三彩之所以呈现多种釉色，是与呈色剂中各种不同的金属氧化物的成分多少有关，如呈色金属铁的氧化物，在褐色(红色)釉中含量为 4.30%，绿色釉中含量 0.20%，黄色釉中含量为 1.50%，蓝色釉中含量为 1.00% 左右；又如呈色金属铜的氧化物，在褐色(红色)釉中含量为 0.31%，绿色釉中含量 0.20%，蓝色釉中含量为 0.30%。不仅如此，化验结果还表

明，即使是同一种釉色的釉药，由于对其色泽深浅浓淡的需要不同，在配制釉药的过程中，呈色剂及其他化学元素的含量比例也不相同。如巩义窑出土的蓝彩片，其呈色剂钴的氧化物的含量是1.03%，而洛阳矿山厂出土的蓝彩片，其含量则是1.09%，铁量增减而显出黄、橙至褐色，铜量的增减产生青、绿之间各种色调。这种情况说明，烧造唐三彩的匠师们为取得多种色釉，不但能够利用不同的呈色剂来表现不同的色彩，而且能以不同的比例来呈现更多的色彩，从而使唐三彩成为万紫千红、绚丽多彩的艺术品。这样复杂的配制釉药的技术，竟在一千多年以前被陶瓷匠师们所熟练掌握，不能不使我们为之惊叹。这是我国古代劳动人民在配制釉药的长期实践中取得的辉煌成果。

唐三彩是釉陶，但又不同于唐代的釉陶：唐三彩是多彩，而釉陶是单色釉；唐三彩是瓷胎（高岭土）和陶胎并存，而釉陶基本上为陶胎；唐三彩胎质密度较大，原料经过淘洗，而釉陶胎质粗糙，气孔明显；唐三彩施釉均匀，而釉陶施釉厚薄不均等。它们既然同属釉陶，必然有其共同之处，如都是有毒的铅釉，造成温度较低、吸收性较强、胎质都有气孔等。唐三彩有的虽然为瓷胎，但不是瓷器：三彩器胎质密度不大，而瓷胎紧密，无吸水性；三彩器釉色缺少透明度，而瓷器透明度强；三彩器烧成温度低，仅800℃左右，而瓷器则为1300℃左右；三彩无清脆之声，而瓷器声音清脆；三彩为多色釉彩，唐代瓷器则为单色釉等。在造型上，三彩器比瓷器丰富。

唐三彩是唐代陶瓷家庭中的一名新成员，是陶瓷百花园中一朵千姿百态的奇葩。这朵奇葩是怎样栽培出来的呢？其渊源很可能就是从汉代绿、黄釉陶器基础上发展而来，在黄、绿釉的基础上经历了彩绘釉陶的过渡阶段。彩绘釉陶就是在釉陶器表面施粉彩，再进行焙烧，使其牢固，这与三彩似有相似之处。而北朝的双彩器，可能就是三彩器的前身。这种双彩器，在北齐墓中多有出土，如李云墓中出土两件黄釉绿彩四系罐，范碎墓中出土白釉绿彩器和淡黄釉加黄、绿二彩器等。可见二彩器很可能是唐三彩釉的雏形，是它们开创了三彩釉的先河。

这朵奇葩何时才真正出现的呢?由于三彩无任何文献可查，只能从考古材料中寻找答案。目前考古资料证实，最早一件唐三彩出现在麟德元年(664年)郑仁泰墓中，是一件带三彩的残器盖。作为完整三彩器，较早的则出土于上元二年(675年)李凤墓中，一件为三彩双联盘，一件为三彩榻，另有十余件三彩残片。这些三彩器，与后来的三彩器比较，已达到比较完善的程度。麟德、上元皆为唐高宗年号，高宗时期，按唐代历史阶段划分，应为初唐时期。可见唐三彩在初唐时已经出现，是唐三彩进程的初期阶段。自三彩出现以后，经历了兴盛和衰落两个阶段。盛唐时期，也就是武则天至唐玄宗开元年间，为唐三彩的兴盛时期；中唐的天宝时期，为唐三彩的没落乃至消亡时期。初唐时期唐三彩，一般以赭褐色、赭黄色釉为主，间以白色或绿色釉彩，采用蘸釉法，点施在器物的肩部；施釉比较粗糙，釉层较厚，流釉现象严重，且成蜡泪状；釉药往往没有烧成，色泽暗淡，釉面不均；器类基本上只有器皿和模型器，种类和数量不多，作为随葬品还不普遍，只是在达官显贵墓中才有为数不多的发现。兴盛时期的唐三彩，色彩齐全，除原有釉色外，新出现了蓝釉和黑釉，形成了多种釉色集于一身的华丽场面；施釉方法从蘸釉法变为混釉法，因而器物釉色光泽晶莹，赋彩自然而不滞板。这时的三彩器除初期的器皿和模型器外，三彩俑异军突起，犹如雨后春笋，凡发现的俑类，全为这个时期的产品，而器皿和模型器种类、数量也是空前增加，可以说三彩品种之多、内容之丰富，是当时任何一种工艺

形式都与之无法相比的。就其生活用具可分为三大类，分别为贮盛器类：计有尊、罐、瓶、壶、樽；饮食用具类：计有碗、盘、杯、钵、盆、盅；卧室书斋器类：计有粉盒、砚台、痰盂、洗、香炉、灯、枕。而模型器除早期的榻外，出现了庭院、房屋、仓库、假山、水池、厕所、柜厨、臼、磨、灶等；当时还出现了玩具类，如口哨、小狗、小狮等。唐三彩中最引人注目，也是最有艺术特色的是这个时期新出现的俑类，出土数量之多、种类之丰富、造型之生动，是任何朝代的同类器物都无法与之比拟的。其中人物类俑有文官、武士、天王、胡人、男仆、女侍、贵妇、牵马牵驼俑、乐舞俑、骑马仪仗俑、骑马狩猎俑、伎乐俑，等等；动物俑类更是应有尽有，有马、骆驼、驴、牛、猴、虎、狗、猪、羊、兔、鸡、鸭、鹅，等等。这时器物上的装饰内容也极为丰富多彩，人物鸟兽、花草蔓枝，在三彩器上都得到了充分的展现。如鹰头壶上的骑马射箭，金鸡独立，模印装铭花纹；盘、枕、罐上的穿云高翔飞雁、鸳鸯踩莲和几何形四瓣划花、回首腾狮以及多种多样的宝相花、牡丹花、团花，无不引人入胜。特别是这个时期用三彩品随葬已非常普遍，从达官显贵到平常百姓家，这可以说是唐三彩最欣欣向荣的时期。唐三彩到了唐玄宗天宝年间，由于受安史之乱的影响，进入了它的没落阶段。安史之乱破坏了稳定的政治局面，破坏了发达的农业和手工业经济，使商品交易停滞，老百姓无钱购买唐三彩，一种缺乏政治环境、经济环境、商品市场、购买力的商品，其结果只有没落，乃至消失，唐三彩当然也逃脱不了这种厄运。没落时期的唐三彩，俑类不见了，仅存的器皿也多是小型者，并由多彩趋向单彩，以同一色彩的浓淡表现其彩花效果，施釉草率，并往往有脱釉迹象，而这时洛阳已不见有唐三彩出土，其他地区虽有发现，也只不过为强弩之末罢了。

唐三彩为何产生于唐代呢?原因是多方面的，唐代是我国封建社会的鼎盛时期，经济、文化都达到了历史空前的高峰。这个时期(前期)，唐王朝的社会是“天下大稳”，“东至于海，南极五岭，皆外户不闭，行旅不带粮，取给于道路焉”。可以说唐三彩是唐代政治、经济、文化高度发展的产物，同时也是我国陶瓷工艺自身发展的必然产物。 唐三彩器的出现表明，我国古代陶瓷工匠对于各种呈色金属原料特性的认识、化学技术的掌握和运用已达到了一个新的水平，唐三彩只不过是北齐彩瓷的直接延续，三彩俑只是借用了唐三彩器皿的施釉方法，在我国古代传统的陶塑工艺基础上发展起来的。宋代文学家苏东坡说：“君子之于学，百工之于艺，自三代历汉，至唐而备矣。”这对于唐三彩出现的社会背景、技术原因是一个恰如其分的评说。

商业贸易和唐代的厚葬之风为唐三彩提供了广阔的市场。洛阳殷商以来向有通衢称号，而隋唐时期洛阳更是“遥山东之贡赋，扼关外之诸侯，直齐梁而驾路，引淮汴而通舟”。可见当时的洛阳，实际上是隋唐两代的交通中心，也是唐当时商业贸易的集散地和国际商业都市，当时隋都城内有三个商业市场，“东市曰大同，北市曰通远，通远市周围六里，其内群国舟船，舳舻万计”；“丰都市周八里，其内一百二十行，三千余肆，市四壁有四百余店，珍奇山积”；诸番和胡客也进市做交易。唐朝洛阳亦有三市，即北市、南市和西市。“西市有邸一百四十一区，经货六十六行”；北市更是“天下之舟船所集，常万余艘填满河路，商贩贸易，车马填塞”。在进行交易中，唐三彩必为其商品之一，全国各地所发现的唐三彩必有洛阳三彩。洛阳是丝绸之路的一个起点，又与海上丝绸之路有十分密切的关系，唐代海上贸易非常发达，中国的丝绸、瓷器历来就是由丝绸之路大批运往海外诸国，唐三彩也不例外，在俄罗斯、伊拉克、伊朗、叙利亚、约旦、埃及、苏丹、意大利、朝鲜、日本等世界诸国都有唐三彩出土，就是极好的证明。国际和国内的商业需要，无疑有助于唐三彩手工业

的发展，而唐代的厚葬之风，更是为唐三彩手工业的发展注入了活力，“王公百官，竞为厚葬，偶人象马，雕锦如生，徒以炫耀路人，本不因心致礼，更相扇慕，破产倾资，风俗流行，遂下兼士庶”。可见厚葬在唐代已普及到寻常百姓家。正是这种厚葬，正是这种破产倾资的厚葬之风，为唐三彩生产提供了广阔的市场和大量的需求。唐三彩很可能是适应这种厚葬风气而兴起的，当然唐三彩作为一种艺术品，也曾受到古代石刻、泥塑、绘画的影响，唐三彩正是从这些艺术中汲取了精华，才成为艺术领域的珍品。

唐三彩是一种集美术与雕塑为一体的艺术品，所取得的成就是喜人的，在生活用具方面是博采众长，罐、塔式罐一类雍容华贵，收放有致；杯盏一类，形态奇特，富有自然情趣，又不失气势。至于胡瓶、胡人尊、狮形杯等，则是三彩工匠们将西域或外国生活用具中一些造型特征，用到三彩制作上，显得华丽，具有异国情调。吸收外来工艺的影响，是唐三彩生活用具与以前其他朝代生活用具很大的不同的原因之一。这些器物从造型到装饰都显示出大唐盛世的气魄。三彩器皿虽然规整统一，但不呆板，是根据器物的特征予以变化，使其美观与和谐联成一个整体，如双螭柄尊，尊柄塑成两条螭龙，龙嘴衔着尊的盘形口，弓身曲尾，弧度很大，既与尊的腹体相称，又富于变化。三彩器皿造型多样，题材广泛：除了吸收各类工艺品的优点外，还摄取了自然界中的生物形象，工匠们在创作中不是生硬地照搬现实中的形象，而是突出物体典型特征。如西安出土的一件山形洗，形体不大，却给人以山势逶迤、层峦叠嶂的感觉，山脚下海棠形的水池，别具匠心。

唐三彩的艺术成就在俑上表现更为突出，它造型生动，惟妙惟肖，形式多样，内容丰富，既有现实生活的真实写照，又有艺术的灵活处理，使其生动活泼，富丽高雅，情趣横生，形成了独特的艺术风格。

唐以前的俑，在内容上多为兵士、乐士、侍女，这种题材的限制，在内容上也就无法反映社会的风貌。而在唐代的俑，题材更广阔，内容更充实，俑人上至达官显贵，下至平民百姓，一一雕塑，而且成功地运用了各种手法，把各个阶层的人物塑造得栩栩如生，恰到好处，并根据不同社会地位、等级，表达出他们特定的情感与特征。唐代匠师们为了表现其贵族妇女体态丰满、艳丽动人的特点，有意加强脸部的体积，使形象更加圆润饱满。为了使面部形象更集中，大胆地将发式进行了高度的概括处理。当时的发式不下百余种，如双高髻、环坠髻、练垂髻、半翻髻、惊鹊髻、单刀髻、两丫髻、单坠髻、鹦鹉髻、螺旋髻等。这些发髻根据贵妇中不同的身材、不同的脸形、不同的形态、不同的姿势、不同的服饰，巧妙地结合在一起，更加显露出贵族妇人、少女的鲜明特征。为衬托贵妇人的高雅气质，匠师们在服装上也做了精心设计，有的窄袖紧身，有的长裙拽地，有的袒胸束腰。匠师们也很注重面部的装饰，装饰有红粉、花细、唇脂、眉黛、额黄等。在形象塑造上也是千姿百态，有的悠闲静坐，若有所思；有的亭亭玉立，裙带生风；有的嬉笑打闹，其乐融融。如洛阳北窑出土的一件女坐俑，朱唇粉面，丰颊腴腮，头梳环髻，身穿袒胸绛色窄袖襦衫，胸束长裙，双手置于胸前，端坐在圆墩上，神气十足，俨然一副贵妇人的形象。由于唐代特有的审美情趣，艺匠们将其比例缩短，用上大下小的体积变化来反映“丰颊体肥”的审美特征。在形式上，艺匠们吸取了宗教雕塑的对称手法，将女立俑的双手举于胸前，藏于袖内，使作品不仅加强了整体感，也加强了生动、活泼的艺术趣味，使人一看便知她们为贵妇人群体。

对于那些峨冠博带的文臣俑，艺师们着意表达他们的道貌岸然，在表情上着力刻画他们端严直立、神情拘谨、温顺虔诚，在上司面前不敢越雷池一步的虚伪面孔：有的两手捧物或两手相交，似乎在窥视上司的脸

色，为上司献策或聆听上司的吩咐；有的挺胸瞪眼，不可一世。匠师们抓住了这个群体的两面嘴脸，将他们的内心世界刻画得淋漓尽致。

对于那些天王俑、武士俑和镇墓兽的形象，匠师们采用夸张的手法，着重从外形上突出表现蹙眉怒目、剑拔弩张、凶神恶煞、气势逼人、不可一世的形态，让人望而生畏，以达到与他们身份相称的效果。

对于那些深目高鼻的胡人牵马牵驼俑、商贩，匠师们主要从面部、帽饰和服饰来刻画他们不同的族属、不同的地域和不同的身份。如关林2号墓出土的一件三彩牵马俑，匠师通过他自信的神态和熟练、内行的牵马姿势，表现出这是一个很有驭马本领的西亚人。仿佛一匹高大矫健的良马顺服地在他身旁嘶鸣，从他脸部造型和体格及衣履装束方面，都体现出西亚人所具有的特点。又如一肩负货袋、手执水壶的胡商俑，由于长途跋涉，且背沉重货物的缘故，显得步履艰难，疲惫不堪。艺匠在这一作品中，以高超的技巧，准确地刻画出波斯商贩的形象。

那些身居下层社会，活跃于舞台上的艺人形象，更是趣味无穷，妙趣横生，艺匠们用粗犷的线条、简单的衣着、扭动的身躯，来表现他们的豪放、无拘无束、活泼乐观的情趣，反映了他们的精神面貌和上层社会人物的根本区别。

在马的塑造上，唐代更是成功之作，既简练概括，又富有浪漫色彩，在汉、唐两代，马的形象塑造达到顶峰。汉马特别厚重，像山一样稳，制作手法大刀阔斧，衣帽取神，着重气势。而唐马俑显得轻松愉快，但又不失凝重之感。在艺术风格上，它不像魏、隋时期所风行的清瘦俊秀，而是饱满圆浑且不流于臃肿，华美富丽又不流于庸俗，装饰品多，而外形仍然清晰明快。三彩马动态丰富，变化多样，有的腾空奔驰，有的腾空马舞，有的缓步徐行，有的昂首嘶鸣，有的低头啃蹄，有的追逐戏耍，无论哪种形态，唐三彩马都给你一种气魄、力量的象征，一种浪漫活泼的感觉。

骆驼的塑造也很成功，一种长途跋涉的交通工具，被人们喻为“沙漠之舟”的骆驼，有的昂首嘶鸣，有的两峰间驮着巨大的行囊，稳步行进在茫茫古道之上、千里戈壁之中，它们这种无所畏惧、坚忍不拔的形象，给人以信心、鼓舞和希望，是中西商旅往来的逼真写照。

唐代匠师们在塑造三彩的形体时，用多种手法，各式各样的装饰纹样，加以装点，使其更具艺术魅力，如马身上的杏叶装饰，就有宝相花、金银花等花样繁多、品种不一、形式各种各样的装饰图案。骆驼身上的行囊包，则有人面、兽面、书箱、行包等多种图案。在器皿的装饰上，内容更为丰富，有人物鸟兽、花草蔓枝等。在雕塑技巧上，手法多样，有划花、堆塑、捏塑、手雕等。

总之，唐三彩艺术上的成就是无籍无名的匠师们，在深入了解、熟悉各阶层人士的生活，洞察各种动物的生活习性，同时不拘一格地借鉴和运用外民族的艺术特点创造出各种不同的，有性格、有情趣的三彩制品。三彩制品是特定时期文化、艺术、科学的结晶，它体现了唐代整个时期民族风格和人们的审美要求。

洛阳和西安同为唐三彩的发源地，同为美术陶瓷工艺中并茂的奇葩。但由于历史、地域的差异，民俗的差异，原料的差异，表现在三彩上也就各有其自己的特色。从釉色和装饰上看，西安的唐三彩器皿一般比洛阳显得清淡素雅，装饰花纹不如洛阳的艳丽繁褥。西安的色彩尚淡，如有一种淡绿色马俑在洛阳至今未见过。而捏塑技法比洛阳采用的要多。洛阳在女俑的塑造方面比较俏丽飘逸，男俑胖瘦得体，武士俑以瘦劲见长；西

安女俑多以丰满艳丽为主，武士则以身形彪壮、短颈粗腰为特征，在釉色上洛阳较之西安更为五彩缤纷，细腻、柔和。在胎质、种类、彩花上也有所不同，西安红泥胎三彩器延续时间较长，而洛阳仅见于三彩的初期。西安三彩制品种类较洛阳为多，如西安的三彩楼阁、亭庭、山峦、水池、骆驼上的伎乐等，这些在洛阳尚未发现。洛阳三彩器皿上多见几何形点彩花纹和重带状花纹，对流釉控制得很好，这种彩花形式产品在西安比较少见。这些差别进一步说明唐三彩并非只有一个产地，而是有多个产地，各产地都有其自身的特征，当然也是相互交流，相互影响，共同发展。

唐三彩既然为一种完美的艺术品，必然受到人们的喜爱和收藏，因而制造假唐三彩也就并非现在才有，而是早已存在。如何辨别唐三彩的真伪呢？要识别假的，也就必须认识真的，就要多到博物馆去认真观察，认识唐三彩的造型、装饰、釉色，了解唐三彩的基本特征。要多翻阅有关唐三彩的图册，必须达到烂熟的程度，自己从中总结出最关键的特征，购置唐三彩时，就用自己总结的特征去加以对照，真假必有结果。

所谓以假乱真，这是不大可能的，形神兼备是唐三彩俑类的主要特点，无论大、小件均能表现出生动的神态，这一点对鉴定真伪十分重要，因为大部分赝品制作比较粗糙，就是较高档的仿品虽然以真品翻模，但其刻画的线条、器物的起伏变化并不是十分清楚，显得较为模糊，神态、表情相差更为明显。

三彩器皿类修坯很细，器形规整，圆器都显得深圆饱满，凡器形不大规则的三彩器皿，应怀疑是否为赝品。

唐三彩釉色变化丰富，绚丽斑斓和釉质清纯明亮是唐三彩的又一主要特点。一般说来，赝品釉色均不及真品绚美、清纯，变化丰富。

唐三彩釉面大多数都有光泽，经过做旧处理的唐三彩釉面多失掉光泽，显得暗而陈旧。

当然识别真伪方法很多，最主要之特点还是在于多研究、多认识真品。

唐三彩这朵陶瓷百花园中的奇葩，在陶瓷舞台上很快就凋谢了，从它出现到凋落，只有百年的短暂历史。虽然时间短暂，但它在唐代的对外文化交流、对外贸易以及在陶瓷工艺上对后世的贡献都是不可低估的。唐三彩产品通过陆上与海上丝绸之路，与丝、瓷器一起运销世界各国。同时在不少唐三彩制品中有的为中亚或西亚的器形，匠师们把它用在唐三彩制作，创造出形制更为别致的三彩，这种别致无疑是中西文化交流的一个缩影。唐三彩不仅将器物远销海外，而且烧造技术也传到了海外，当时埃及、朝鲜、日本诸国都纷纷加以仿制。朝鲜烧制出“新罗三彩”，日本烧制出“奈良”三彩，凡此种种，无一不是友好交往、文化交流的见证。在国内的“宋三彩”和“辽三彩”也是唐三彩的继承和延续。而宋代以后的各种各样低温色釉上彩瓷，大部分都是在唐三彩陶工艺基础上发展起来的。因此可见，唐三彩在陶瓷工艺上对后世做出了重大贡献。

作 者

参考资料

李知宴：《唐三彩生活用具》　魏俊：《谈唐三彩的艺术纵横》
韩于西：《洛阳唐三彩纵横》　洛阳博物馆：《洛阳唐三彩》

INTRODUCTION

Tang Tricolor products were firstly discovered in Luoyang. A number of tombs of the Tang Dynasty were excavated under the construction of the Lianyungang–Lanzhou Railway, at the foot of the Mangshan Mountain in the North of Luoyang, in the late twenties of the last century. A large quantity of funeral objects including Tang Tricolor products were excavated. From then on, Tang Tricolor products which had been buried for more than 1000 years, could see light once more. The undocumented multi–colored pottery, discovered in the ancient city of Luoyang, was named Tang Tricolor. The astonishing discovery caused a sensation throughout the country, startled the archaeological circle, the antique circle and the collection circle in the world. The people in the worldwide art circle rushed into Beijing and Luoyang to search for and purchase these gems even at a high price. The ancient capital which had been forgotten for a long time recalled all the people's great attention and became famous for the beauty and richness of the historical relics. The discovery of Tomb of Jincun established the position of Luoyang in the archaeological circle, the antique circle and the collection circle.

Luoyang is not only the first place where Tang Tricolor products were discovered, but also the birthplace of Tang Tricolor. On one hand, it was unimaginable to carry so many and various Tang Tricolor products from other places as they're fragile. Therefore, they were mainly made of local resources and sold in local areas.Of course，some of them may be made in Xi' an, another center of Tang Tricolor. On the other hand, after the establishment of the Tang Dynasty, the stable politics, the developed economy and the flourishing trade in Luoyang provided a guarantee and a market for

Tang Tricolor products. Moreover, the pottery handicraft in Luoyang had a long history and delicate techniques. As far as porcelain was concerned, the blue ones could be produced well 2000 years earlier than Tang Tricolor products in Luoyang .And the low-fired glazed pottery appeared as early as in the Han Dynasty, based on the abundant raw materials in Luoyang. All of these conditions showed that Tang Tricolor products could be made in Luoyang. Furthermore, the kiln sites were found in Gongyi County, Luoyang (today'sHuangye Village in Gongyi). The variety and roughcast of the Tri-colored pottery in this place belong to the same category as that in Luoyang. Therefore, Tang Tricolor products were made in Gongyi County, Luoyang. We are sure there must be other Tang Tricolor sites around Luoyang, although we haven't found them up to now, because Tang Tricolor products made here could not meet the demands in Luoyang. Besides, Luoyang as well as Xi' an was the center of producing Tang Tricolor products. As the birthplace of Tang Tricolor, they must have showed up in the same period. Tang Tricolor products were discovered not only in Luoyang and Xi' an, but also unearthed in other areas, such as the South, the North, the Northwest, the Southwest and the Northeast of China. Tang Tricolor products found in these areas have their own distinctive features with different styles from those found in Luoyang and Xi'an. Thus,it's undoubted that Tang Tricolor products found in these areas were also made of the local raw materials, based on the local techniques. It is obvious that their production techniques inevitably be influenced by those from Luoyang and Xi' an, the earliest and productive places for Tang Tricolor products.

Tang Tricolor products are a kind of low-fired lead glazed pottery, mainly made up of three colors. They are mostly yellow, green, white color, or yellow, green, reddish brown color, in addition to dark green, light green, emerald green, blue, brown color, etc. Therefore, Tang Tricolor is the general name of multi-colored glazed pottery. The multi-colored glaze depends on the ingredients of various metal oxides in the colorant agent. For example, the iron oxide occupies 4.30 percent in the brown glaze, 0.20 percent in the green glaze, 1.50 percent in the yellow glaze, and about 1.00 percent in the blue glaze. While the copper oxide occupies 0.31 percent in the brown glaze, 0.2 percent in the green glaze, and 0.30 percent in the blue glaze. In addition, the results of chemical examinations show that the proportions of colorant agent to other chemical elements are different in the same glaze due to the different needs for dark or light color in the process of prescription. For instance, the blue glazed wares, unearthed in Gongyi, contain 1.03 percent of the cobalt oxide, while 1.09 percent of cobalt oxide in those from Luoyang mining factories. The color can vary from yellow, orange to brown with different amounts of iron, and from blue to green with amounts of copper, that is, Tang Tricolor craftsmen could make use of different proportions of the colorant agents to obtain more colors, and developed Tang Tricolor into a

colorful and brilliant work of art. It's a miracle that such complicated prescription techniques were applied skillfully a thousand years ago, which were the brilliant achievements of the ancient Chinese people through a long period of practice in the process of prescription.

Tang Tricolor products belong to the glazed pottery, but a little different from that of the Tang Dynasty. As a mixture of porcelain and pottery, Tang Tricolor is multi-colored while the glazed pottery is primarily mono-colored; Tang Tricolor is delicate with high density, even glaze and panned raw materials, while the glazed pottery is rough with obvious gas holes and in poor quality. On the other hand, they also have something in common. Both of them contain poisonous lead glaze and gas holes with better absorbent function, made at a low-fired temperature. Yet Tang Tricolor is different from porcelain that is of higher density and nonabsorbent quality. The former, fired at the lower temperature, around 800℃, looks more transparent and sounds clearer than the latter, fired at the temperature of 1300℃. In addition, Tang Tricolor is always in various glaze and shape, whereas porcelain is in mono-colored glaze and dull shape.

As a new member of porcelain and pottery, Tang Tricolor can date back to the green, yellow glaze in the Han Dynasty. It underwent the transition of the painting glazed pottery, which is painted with colored powder and fired to be solid. The Tri-colored glazed wares may be derived from the double painted wares of the North Dynasty. Double painted wares were mostly from the tombs of the Northern Qi Dynasty, such as two jars in yellow glaze with green color from Tomb of Li Yun, the ware in white glaze with green color and in light yellow glaze with yellow and green color unearthed from Tomb of Fan Sui, etc. So Tang Tricolor probably originated from the double painted wares.

As to the exact time for the existence of Tang Tricolor, no documents but the archaeological materials can be consulted. At present, it has been confirmed that the earliest Tang Tri-colored ware is a damaged cover in three colors, found in Tomb of Zheng Rentai in the first year of Linde Period (in 664). A duplex tray and a couch are the earlier complete tri-colored wares, made in the second year of Shangyuan Period (in 675). They were discovered in Tomb of Li Feng together with over ten broken tri-colored pieces, perfect compared with the later wares. As Linde and Shangyuan were both the reign title of Emperor Gaozhong of the Tang Dynasty, Tang Tricolor obviously emerged in the early Tang Dynasty, which went through prosperity and decline. The flourishing Tang Dynasty lasted from the reign of Emperess Wu Zetian to Kaiyuan Period of Emperor Xuanzhong, descending in Tianbao Period of the mid-Tang Dynasty. In the early Tang Dynasty, the tri-colored wares were primarily in reddish, brown and reddish yellow glaze, sometimes in white or green glaze. The thick glaze, dipped roughly on the shoulder of a ware, looks like tears of a burning candle, with uneven layer for failure in

tfiring and in dark color. The variety and the quantity of Tang Tricolor products were so small that they were not commono be buried as funeral objects, only found in official and noble tombs. While in the flourishing Tang Dynasty, they were in full colors.The addition of blue and black glazes made them look more magnificent. And the painting method, changing from the dipping skill to the mixing skill, created a natural lustrous color. Besides the vessel and mould wares of the early time, the tri-colored figures sprang up like the bamboo shoots after a spring rain. With the increasing number and variety, they couldn't be matched by any contemporary handicrafts. In terms of the household utensils, it can be divided into three categories. They are respectively the vessels including copper cup , pots, bottles, kettles, wine goblets; the diet appliances including bowls, sets, cups, basins, handleless cup; the bedroom and study apparatuses including powder boxes, ink stones, the spittoon, rinsing tray, the incense burners, lights, pillows; the model implements such as the courtyard , building , storehouse , rockery , pool , toilet , chest kitchen , joint of bones , mill , cooking stove,etc. besides the early couch; and even the toy wares, like whistle, puppy, small lion, etc. The most attraction lies in the figures of this period. They were of unprecedented variety in shape, vast in number and vivid in image. Human figures range from officials, armored warriors, heavenly kings, the non — Han nationalities Living in north and west in ancient times, male servants, maids, noble ladies, musicians and dancers, figures leading a horse or a camel, figures riding for ceremony or hunting, etc. Whereas animal figures cover horses, camels, donkeys, monkeys, tigers, dogs, pigs, sheep, rabbits, chickens, ducks, gooses, etc. And the decorations on the wares found full expression in humans,animals, flowers and vines, such as the riding and hunting, golden cock standing on one leg, and the decorative inscription pattern on the eagle-headed kettle; the soaring wild goose, the mandarin duck stepping on the lotus, the four-petal flower shaped in geometry, looking back at the prancing lion as well as alluring magnolia, peonies in the trays, pillows and pots. All of them appeal to attention to appreciate. It was very prevalent to take tri-colored wares as funerary objects in this period, ranging from the mass to noble families. So Tang Tricolor entered the most flourishing stage. However, it began to decline from Tianbao Period of Emperor Xuanzhong, because An Shi Rebellion spoiled the stable politics and business, destroyed the developed agriculture and handicraft, made the commercial trade standstill, and common people had no money to buy these wares. Lack of political setting, commercial market, and purchasing power, Tang Tricolor automatically went downhill and even came to extinction. The figures among Tang Tricolor products disappeared in this declining period. The only existing household utensils are in small size and mono-colored glaze. The rash painting cause the glaze to peel away. Moreover, Tang Tricolor products of this period were never discovered in Luoyang. Although unearthed occasionally in other areas,

they were simply like an arrow at the end of its flight.

There are various reasons for Tang Tricolor created in the Tang Dynasty. But most of all, the Tang Dynasty is the peak period of politics, economy and cultures in feudalist society. So Tang Tricolor is the inevitable outcome of the high development of politics, economy,cultures as well as ceramics handicraft. They indicate the ancient Chinese craftsmen had a new understanding of the nature of various raw metal materials, and could apply the chemistry technology skillfully. And they are just the direct continuation of colored ceramics of the Northern Qi Dynasty. Whereas the tri-colored figures developed on the basis of nothing more than traditional pottery sculpturing techniques and the glaze painting skills applied in the tri-colored household utensils.

Business and trade along with the tendency of lavish funerals provided a broad market for Tang Tricolor products. Since the Shang Dynasty, Luoyang has been called "Thorough fare". However, in the Sui and Tang dynasties, Luoyang actually served as the traffic center and the collecting and distributing center of commerce and international trade city. In the Sui Dynasty , there were three markets in Luoyang, named Fengdu market in the east, Datong market in the South, and Tongyuan market in the North of the city. Tongyuan could accommodate thousands of boats. Fengdu is the main place for trading with the non—Han nationalities living in north and west in ancient times. In the Tang Dynasty, there were also three markets in Luoyang, named North market, South market and West market, where Tang Tricolor products became a necessity in trading. So Tang Tricolor products made in Luoyang can be unearthed all over the country. As another starting point of the Silk Road, Luoyang was closely connected with the Silk Road by sea. With the developed overseas trade in the Tang Dynasty, Chinese silk and porcelain were carried in bulk to overseas countries by the Silk Road, with no exception of Tang Tricolor products. The unearthed Tang Tricolor products serve as the best certification in many countries of the world, such as Russia, Iraq, Iran, Syria, Jordan, Egypt, Sudan, Italy, Korea and Japan, etc. Both the International and domestic commercial demand undoubtedly enhanced the development of the Tang Tricolor handicraft. Moreover, the tendency of lavish funerals provided broad markets and stimulated great demand for Tang Tricolor products. As a work of art, Tang Tricolor products were influenced by ancient inscription, clay sculpturing and painting, and became the treasure in the field of art.

Tang Tricolor is a mixture of painting and sculpturing, which has reached a gratifying achievement in household utensils. Pots, tower-shaped pots and the like are magnificent and elegant; cups and lamps are odd and peculiar, full of natural sentiment and momentum. As for the vases and vessels used by the non — Han nationalities living in north and

west in ancient times and the lion-shaped cup, absorbing the Western styles, are splendid and colorful. The applicationof alien techniques is one of the most important differences between household utensils of the Tang Dynasty and those of other dynasties. These appliances showed the prosperity of the Tang Dynasty both in design and decoration. These utensils, standardized but flexible, vary with their own eatures, combining beauty with harmony properly, such as double-handled vessel shaped in Loong. These utensils in various shapes take in the excellences of all handicrafts on the basis of the natural image of living beings, stressing typical features. For example, a small mountain-shaped rinsing tray , unearthed in Xi'an , offers a scene of serpentine mountains rising one upon another, with a unique crab-shaped pool on the foot .

The artistic achievements of Tang Tricolor prominently consist in figures, which were sculpted vividly and absolutely lifelike with various forms and rich models. As a true portrayal of real life, Tang Tricolor appears vivid, elegant, and interesting, forming a unique artistic style.

Most of the figures are confined to the shapes of soldiers, musicians, and attendants before the Tang Dynasty. This restriction can not reflect the social styles and features. However, the figures of the Tang Dynasty cover a wide range from high nobility to common people, moreover, various skills were successfully applied to sculpture figures from all walks of life and display the specific emotions and features. Craftsmen of the Tang Dynasty intentionally made the facial shapes plump and round to show the chubbiness and flamboyance of noblewomen. In order to focus on the facial images, they also boldly generalized hair styles from over hundred hairdos, such as double bun, coil, folded bun, magpie-shaped bun, blade-shaped bun, parrot-shaped bun, spiral bun and so on. These hairdos could match different figures, facial shapes, postures, and costumes, manifesting the distinct features of noblewomen and young girls. In order to set off the elegance of noblewomen, craftsmen designed the clothes meticulously, some of which are close fitting, some narrow-sleeved, some long dressing, or bare-chested with waist band. The facial dress-up included lipstick and different powder for cheeks, eyebrows and temples. Varied in mould shaping, some were leisurely sitting, seeming lost in thought; some were fair, slim and graceful, with their belts flowing, some were laughing and maltreating for fun. For example, the seated female figure unearthed in the North kiln of Luoyang, wore bare-chested, crimson, narrow-sleeve jacket and long shirt as well as lipstick, pink face, chubby cheek, central bun. Liftting her hands in front of chest and sitting on a round cushion. Obviously, she was a confidently noblewoman. Due to the special aesthetic sentiment of the Tang Dynasty, craftsmen shortened the proportion and used the change of volume to reflect the aesthetic feature of chubby cheek and

body. Formally, assimilating the symmetry of religious sculpture, craftsmen made sitting female figures put their hands in front of chest, and standing ones hide their hands in the sleeves. This strengthens the sense of unitary, and vivid, lively artistic taste of the figures that can be easily identified as noblewomen.

As for knowledgeable official figures with high topped hat and broad waist band, craftsmen took pains to sculpt their sanctimoniousness, and depict the sedateness, formality of their facial expression, gentleness and godliness. Some held objects in both hands or crossed their hands, seemed to peer at their nibs, offering suggestions and listening respectfully, some threw a chest and stared, extremely arrogant. Catching hold of their double characters, craftsmen depicted their inside world fully.

As to the heavenly king figures, warriors and animality patrons in tomb, craftsmen adopt the exaggerative tactics, especially stressing the facial expressions and postures to achieve the effects of matching their identity.

As to the horse-leading or camel-leading figures of the non — Han nationalities living in north and west in ancient times with deep eyes and high nose, craftsmen mainly portrayed the different races, regions and identities from faces, hat decorations and dressings. Such as the tri-colored horse-leading figures unearthed from Tomb Guanlin No. 2 , crafts-men depicted it as a West Asian with confident air and skillful postures of leading a horse. Another businessman figure of the non-Han nationalities living in north and west in ancient times, bearing the goods bag and holding the kettle in his hand, seems to walk through hardships exhausted.

The music players, in a lower state of the society but active on the stage, were even full of wits and humor. Artisans expressed their uninhibited character, unrestrained spirit, and optimistic appeal with bold and vigorous lines, simple clothes and swaying bodies, which embodies the entertainers'basic differences in mental outlook from the people of the upper state of the society.

Horses were shaped successfully in romantic colors to reach the peak especially in the Han and Tang dynasties. The horse figures of the Han Dynasty were emphasized on the momentum of mountains with the drastic means. While horse figures of the Tang Dynasty seem to be not only brisk and light, but also dignified and calm. From the prospect of artistic style, they are plump but not obese, magnificent but not vulgar, different from those of the Wei and Sui dynasties, when leanness and delicacy were popular in many decorations and bright looks. Tri-colored horses are dynamic and varied. Some were running highly to the sky, some dancing to the sky and some ambling along, while others are raising their heads and neighing, some bowing their heads to nibble hoofs, some chasing to tease. So the Tri-colored horses of the

Tang Dynasty, in whatever posture, serve as the symbol of strength and lovely romance.

Meanwhile, the shape of camels is also a great success. Camel, known as "The boat of desert", is a means of transportation for people to make a long and arduous journey. Some of these figures are raising their heads and whinnying, while some are carrying huge traveling bags between the humps, marching forward on the boundless ancient way throughout the Gobi desert steadily.Their fearless and persistent images can not only arouse belief,courage and hope in people,but also record the real business and trade between China and the West.

In modeling the shapes of Tang Tricolor products, craftsmen could use a variety of ornaments for decoration skillfully. For instance, the Apricot leaf decorations on the horses are varied. Such as magnolia, honeysuckle and so on, the patterns of which are different and diverse. The designs of the traveling bags are of different kinds, too. There are pictures like the shape of human or animal face, book and traveling bag. Rich and varied decorations are also inlaid on the wares, figures and objects, birds and beasts, flowers and grass, branches and tendrils, etc. Additionally, there are varieties of skills in sculpturing, such as incised design,embossment,etc.

Anyway, Tang Tricolor was achieved by those anonymous handicraftsmen, who were familiar with different habits of animals and see into one's heart. They boldly made full use of artistic characteristics of other nations as references to create diverse interests. Tang Tricolor is the rich fruits of cultures, arts and science during a special time. It embodies both the social customs of the Tang Dynasty and people's aesthetic need.

Both Luoyang and Xi' an, are the places of origin for Tang Tricolor. But owing to the divergences in histories and regions, customs and resources, they reflect their own characters on the tricolors. The glaze of the tri-colored wares in Xi' an seems delicate and elegant, as the color is lighter, for example, a light green-colored glazed horse figure hasn't been found in Luoyang so far.On the other hand, the decorative patterns are not so garish and over elaborate as that of Luoyang. And nipping skills are applied a lot more than that of Luoyang. Luoyang female figures are pretty graceful and elegant, male figures are neither too fat nor too thin, and the warrior figures are known for their thinness and vigor. Yet, Xi' an female figures found in Xi' an are mainly plump and gorgeous; warrior figures are hefty with short necks and brawny waists. As to the glaze color, figures in Luoyang appear more colorful, exquisite and lustrous. Diversities also can be found in the quality of roughcasts, varieties and colorful veins. The red roughcasts of Tang Tricolor in Xi'an lasted for a long time, yet the ones in Luoyang only existed during the initial stages of Tang Tricolor time. Xi'an has more kinds of the tri-colored pottery than Luoyang, like tri-colored towers, pavilions, georgettes, mountains, ponds, camel-riding

musicians were discovered in Xi' an, but not yet discovered in Luoyang. Besides, Tang Tricolor products in Luoyang generally have geometrical spots and repeated coagulum patterns which are rare in Xi'an, the floating glaze controlled very well. All of these disparities further show that Tang Tricolor is derived from not one place but many other places. Each of them has its own features.They influence each other and develop well together.

Now that Tang Tricolor is a perfect work of art, inevitably it will be loved and collected by people. So the forging of it has existed for long. In order to tell the real from the fake, it is necessary to go frequently to the museum, examine carefully and recognize the basic features of Tang Tricolor products well from moulds, decorations and glaze. Then books about Tang Tricolor products are also a good choice. Read them a lot and try to keep them in mind and conclude the crucial features of Tang Tricolor products from the books. When buying the wares, we can use our experience and knowledge to make a contrast.

It is impossible to mistake the false for the true if the identifying methods be grasped. The main characteristics of Tang Tricolor is the combination of appearance and spirit. No matter how big or small, their miens are vivid. This point is important when judging the real from false. Most art forgeries are made coarsely. The differences in miens and looks of the wares tend to be obvious, as the rising and falling of lines of high-level imitations attend to be vague.

The moulds for casting of Tang Tricolor products are exquisite. Their shapes are standardized. They look perfectly round, full and regular. So those without a standard shape should be doubted whether as art forgeries.

That the glaze of Tang Tricolor products looks transparent, colorful and varied, is another primary feature of its own.

Most Tang Tricolor products are of luster on the smooth surface. While those fake ones look old and dark for the lack of luster.

Of course, there are many other methods of telling the real from the fake, the basic one of which consists in researching and identifying more about the real.Tang Tricolor has gone through a history of only 100 years since it came into being, making an immeasurable contribution to the external culture exchanges, foreign trade and business as well as ceramic industry. Through the Silk Road on the continent and by sea, Tang Tricolor products are sold abroad with silk and porcelain. At the same time, artists applied the molds of Middle-Asia and Western Asia in the production of Tang Tricolor products. So they created more unique tri-colored wares, which are undoubtedly an epitome of the culture exchange between China and the West. Tang Tricolor products were sold abroad and the fired skills were spreading all over the world. Egypt, Korea and Japan imitated in succession and created "the New Luo tri-colored pottery" in Korea, "the

Nara tri-color pottery"in Japan, etc. and all of them witness the friendly communication and culture exchanges between each other. The tri-colored wares in the Song and Liao dynasties both carry on the style of Tang Tricolor, becausethe various low-fired glazed pottery from the Song Dynasty were mostly developed on the basis of the tri-colored handicrafts of the Tang Dynasty. Thus it is clear that Tang Tricolor makes a great and profound contribution in the ceramic techniques.

author

Reference Books

Household Utensils of Tang Tricolor by Li Zhiyan

On the Arts of Tang Tricolor by Wei Jun

Perspectives on Tang Tricolor by Han Yuxi

Tang Tricolor in Luoyang by Luoyang Museum

目 录
Contents

人俑

男俑

三彩文官俑
唐代
陶器
一级文物
通高112厘米

Tri-colored figure of civil official
Tang Dynasty
Pottery
Fist-class cultural relics
112 cm in height

三彩鸟冠文官俑

陶器

一级文物

宽25.5厘米

厚23.5厘米　高113厘米

Tri-colored figure of civil ofticial with a cockscomb shaped crown

Pottery

First-class cultural relics

25.5 cm in width

23.5 cm in thickness　113 cm in height

三彩文官俑

陶器
二级文物
高92厘米
最宽19厘米　厚18.5厘米

Tri-colored figure of civil official
Pottery
Second-class cultural relics
92 cm in height
19 cm in width　18.5 cm in thickness

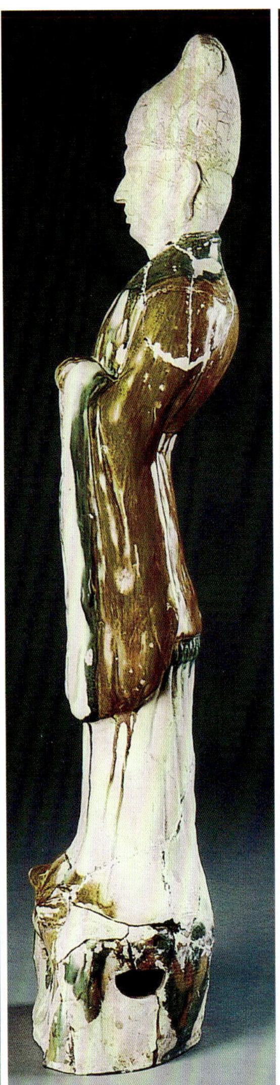

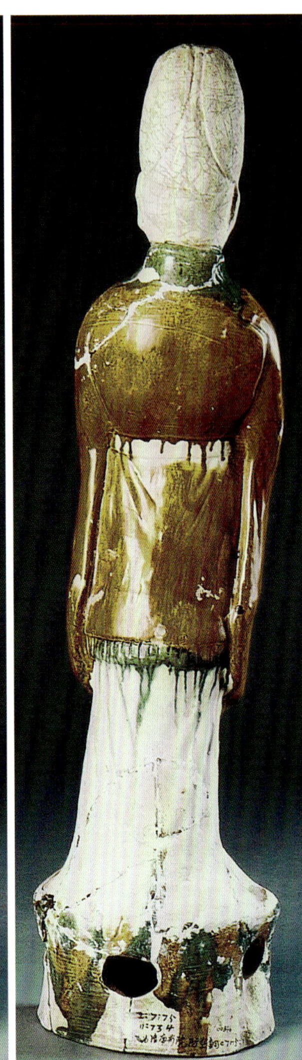

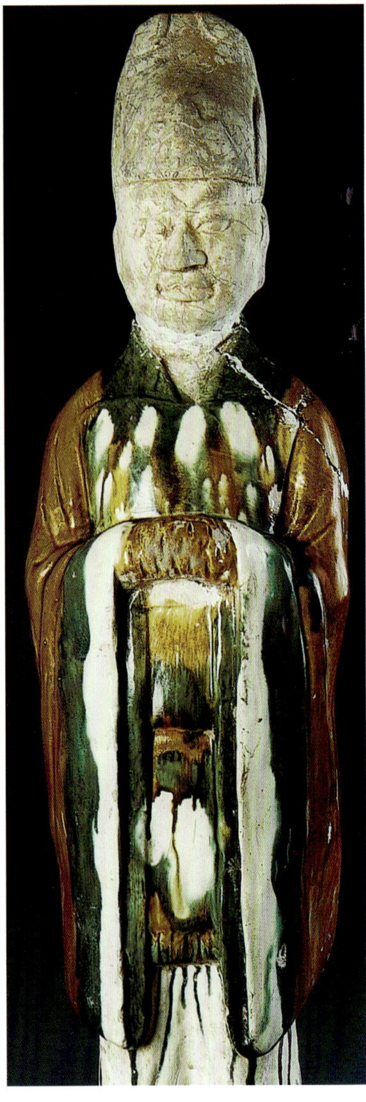

三彩文官俑
唐代
陶器
二级文物
高77.5厘米

Tri-colored figure of civil official
Tang Dynasty
Pottery
Second-class cultural relics
77.5 cm in height

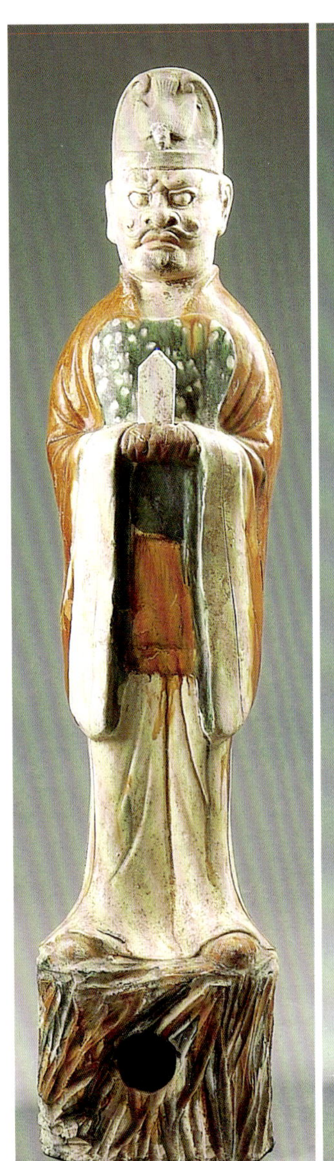

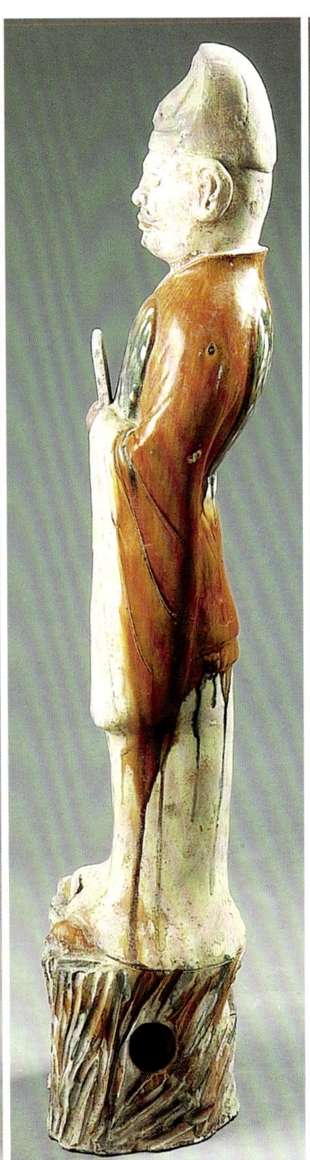

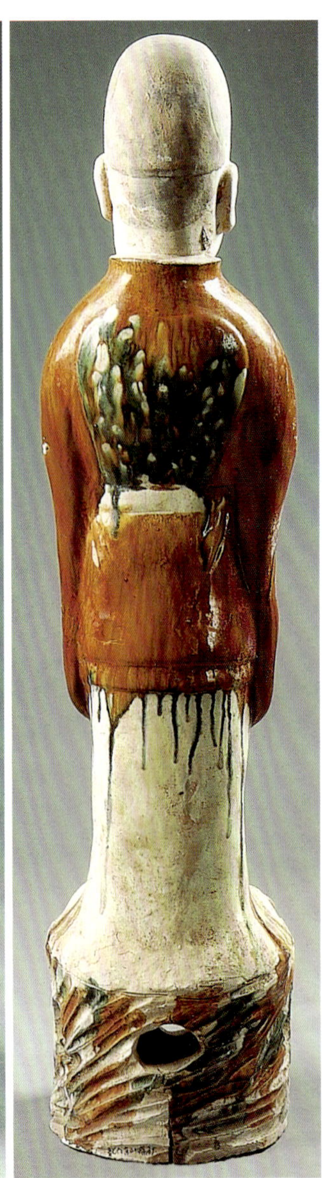

三彩文官俑

唐代 | Tri-colored figure of civil official

陶器 | Tang Dynasty

二级文物 | Pottery

高87厘米 | Second-class cultural relics

87 cm in height

三彩文官俑

唐代 Tri-colored figure of civil official

陶器 Tang Dynasty

Pottery

二级文物 Second-class cultural relics

高53厘米 53 cm in height

三彩束发冠文官俑

唐代
陶器
一级文物
高107厘米

Tri-colored figure of civil ofticial with hair tied
Tang Dynasty
Pottery
First-class cultural relics
107 cm in height

三彩文吏俑
唐代
陶器
二级文物
高 67 厘米

Tri-colored figure of government clerk
Tang Dynasty
Pottery
Second-class cultural relics
67 cm in height

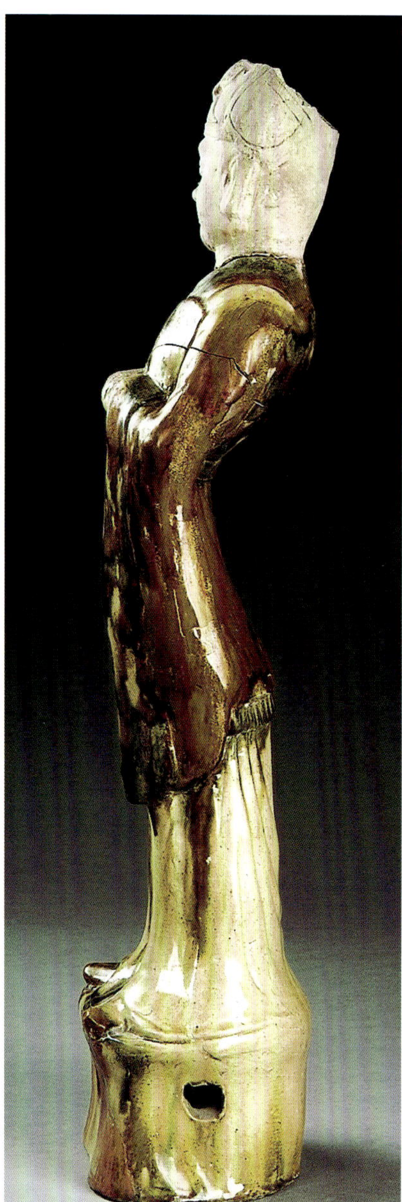

三彩文官俑

陶器

二级文物

纵 16.5 厘米　横 14.2 厘米

高 72 厘米

Tri–colored figure of civil official

Pottery

Second–class cultural relics

16.5 cm in length　14.2 cm in width

72 cm in height

三彩文官俑

唐代	Tri-colored figure of civil official
陶器	Tang Dynasty
二级文物	Pottery
	Second-class cultural relics
纵 14.5 厘米　横 14 厘米	14.5 cm in length　14 cm in width
高 68.3 厘米	68.3 cm in height

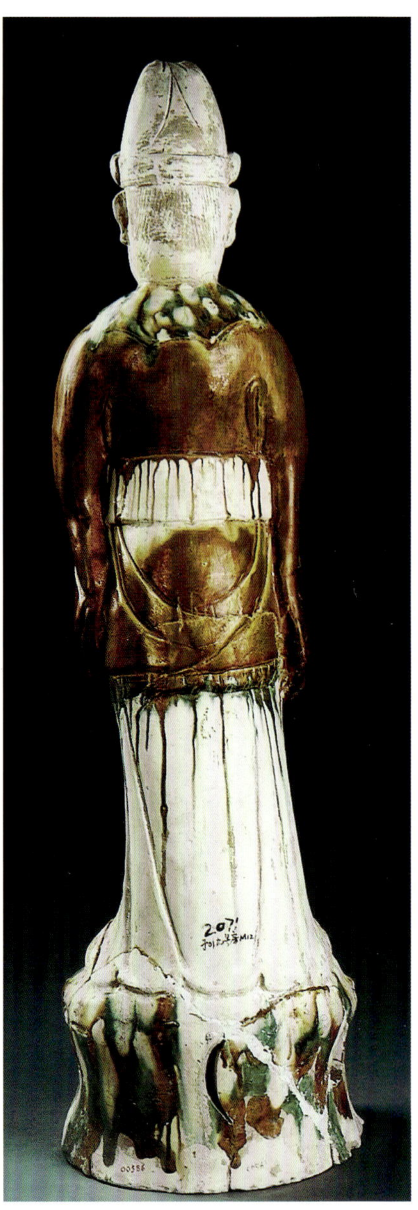

三彩文官俑

陶器

二级文物

纵 24 厘米　横 18 厘米

高 84 厘米

Tri-colored figure of civil official

Pottery

Second-class cultural relics

24 cm in length　18 cm in width

84 cm in height

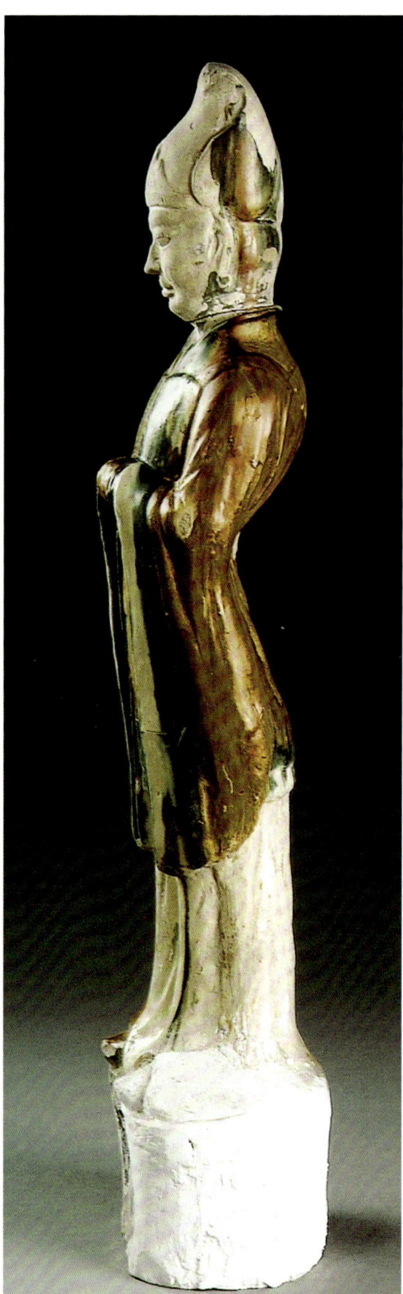

三彩文官俑

唐代	Tri-colored figure of civil official
陶器	Tang Dynasty
二级文物	Pottery
	Second-class cultural relics
纵 18.5 厘米　横 14 厘米	18.5 cm in length　14 cm in width
高 79 厘米	79 cm in height

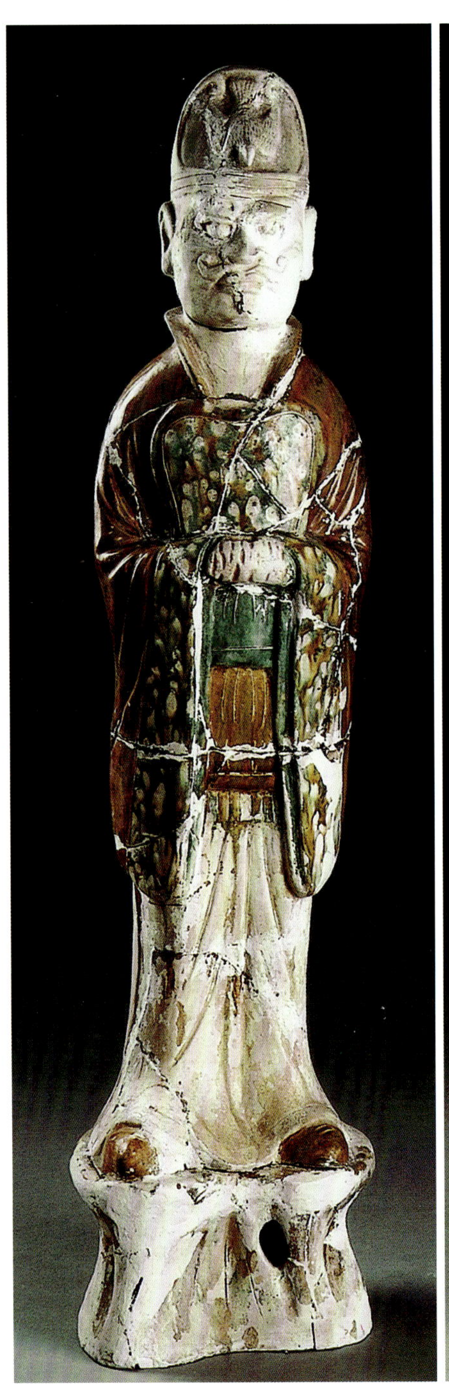

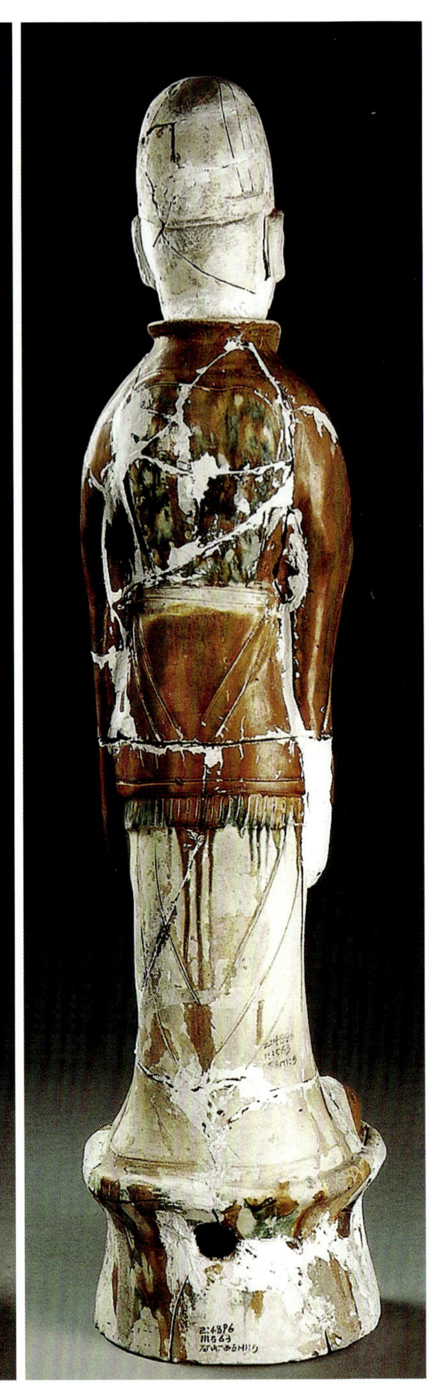

三彩文官俑
唐代
陶器
二级文物
纵20厘米　横15厘米
高87.5厘米

Tri-colored figure of civil official
Tang Dynasty
Pottery
Second-class cultural relics
20 cm in length 15 cm in width
87.5 cm in height

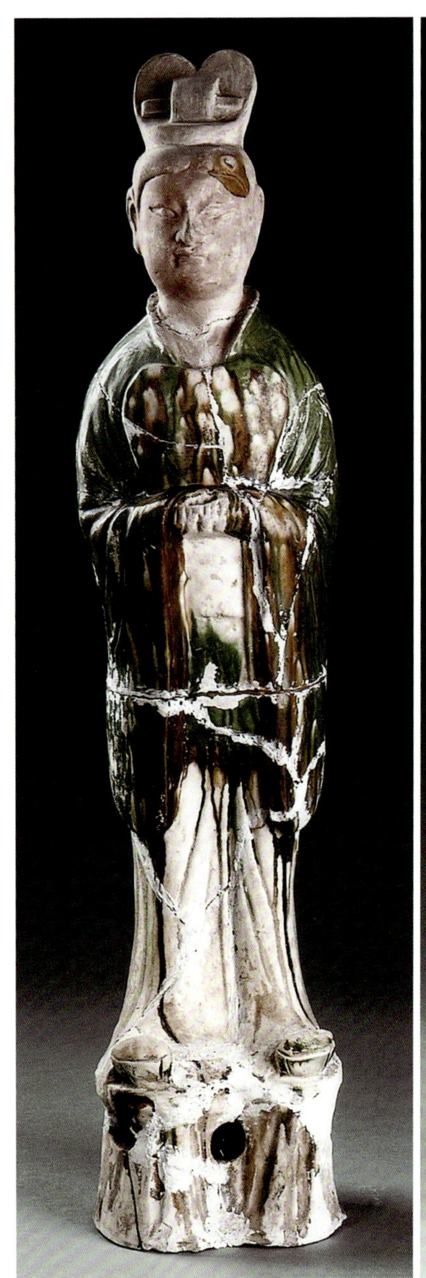

三彩文官俑

唐代
陶器
二级文物
纵 19 厘米　横 16.5 厘米
高 85 厘米

Tri-colored figure of civil official
Tang Dynasty
Pottery
Second-class cultural relics
19 cm in length　16.5 cm in width
85 cm in height

三彩男伶俑

唐代	Tri-colored actor figure
陶器	Tang Dynasty
二级文物	Pottery
高39厘米	Second-class cultural relics
	39 cm in height

三彩文官俑

唐代	Tri-colored figure of civil official
陶器	Tang Dynasty
二级文物	Pottery
	Second-class cultural relics
纵 17.8 厘米　横 12.7 厘米	17.8 cm in length　12.7 cm in width
高 67.5 厘米	67.5 cm in height

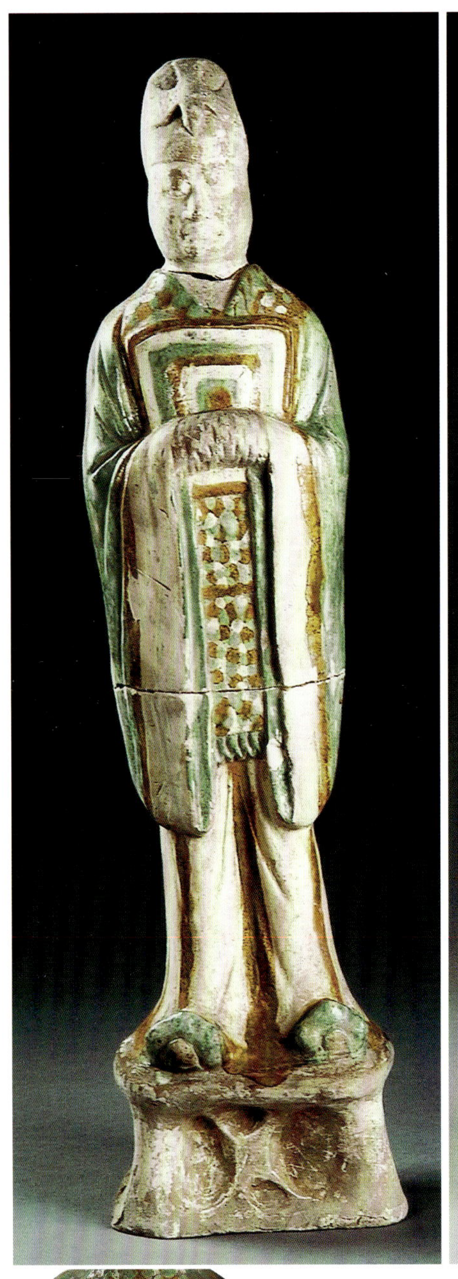

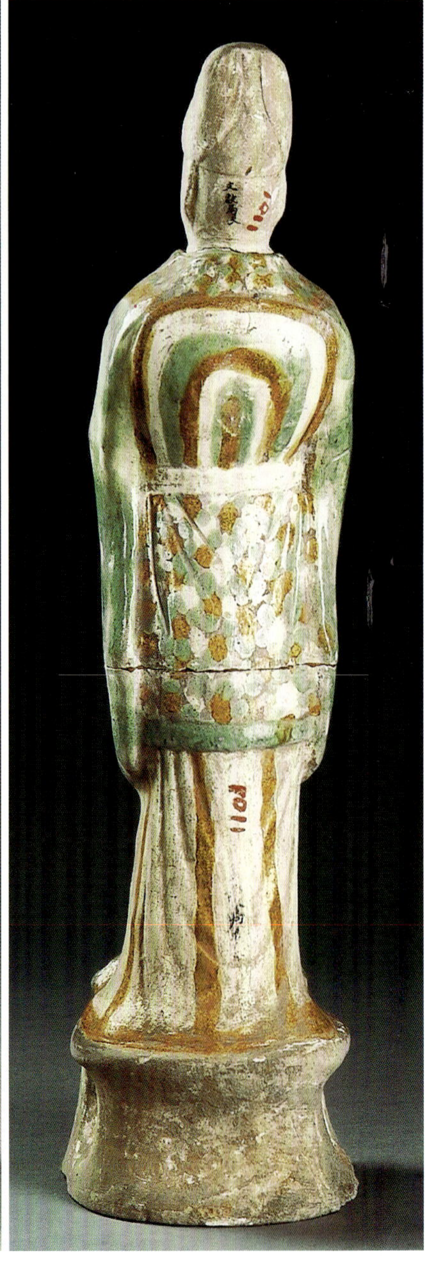

三彩文官俑

唐代 Tri-colored figure of civil official

陶器 Tang Dynasty

二级文物 Pottery

Second-class cultural relics

纵 19.5 厘米　横 15.5 厘米 19.5 cm in length 15.5 cm in width

高 75 厘米 75 cm in height

三彩武士俑

唐代	Tri-colored warrior figure
陶器	Tang Dynasty
	Pottery
二级文物	Second-class cultural relics
高 42 厘米　纵 20 厘米	42 cm in height　20 cm in length

三彩文官俑

唐代 Tri-colored figure of civil official

陶器 Tang Dynasty

二级文物 Pottery

Second-class cultural relics

纵24厘米 横18.5厘米 24 cm in length 18.5 cm in width

高90.5厘米 90.5 cm in height

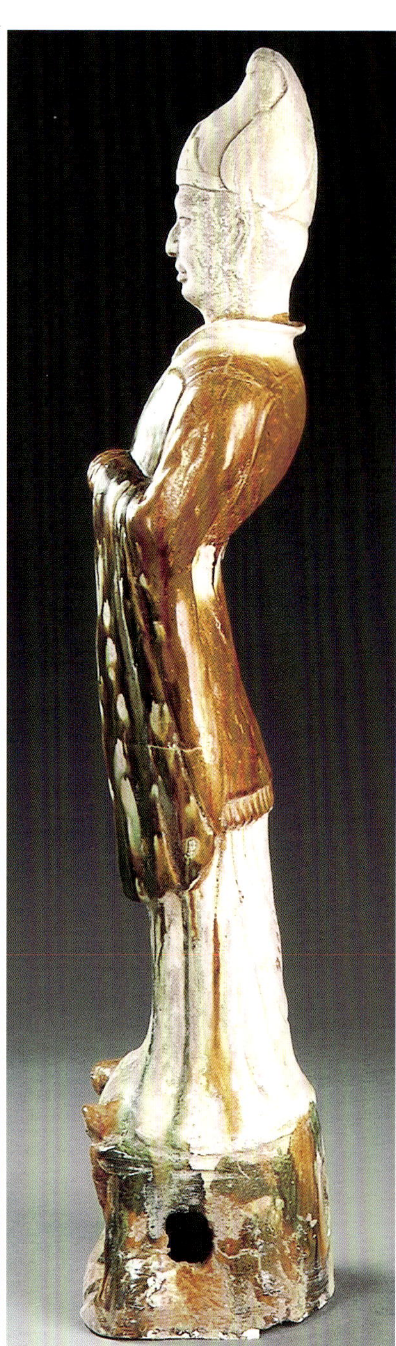

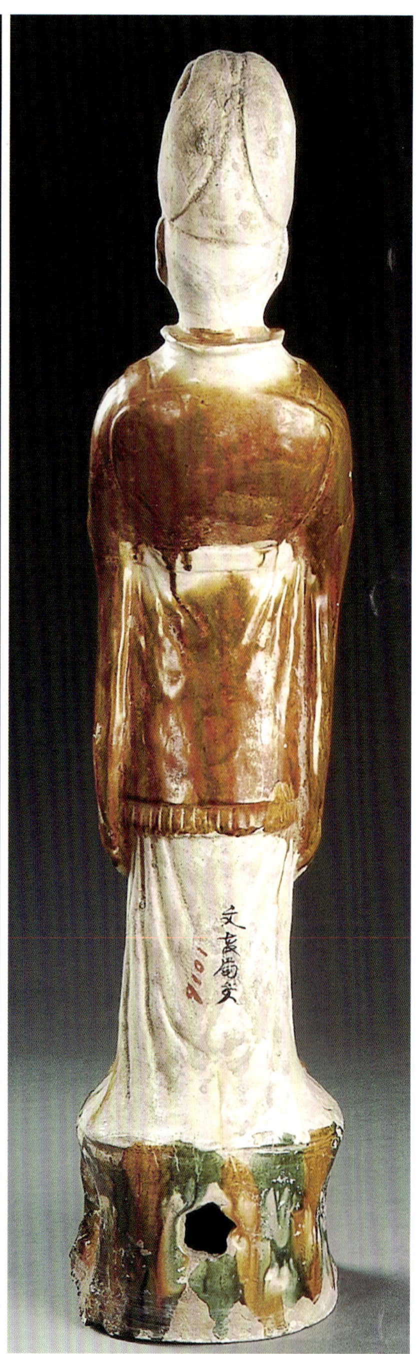

三彩文官俑

唐代

陶器

二级文物

纵 11.5 厘米　横 17 厘米

高 73 厘米

Tri-colored figure of civil official

Tang Dynasty

Pottery

Second-class cultural relics

11.5 cm in length　17 cm in width

73 cm in height

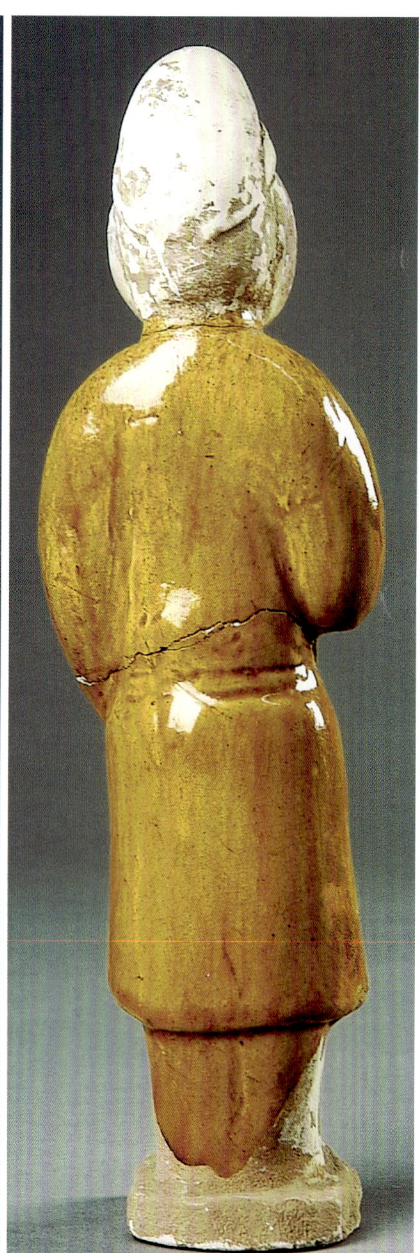

黄釉男胡俑

唐代
陶器
二级文物
高30厘米

Yellow-glazed male figure of the non-Han nationalities
Tang Dynasty
Pottery
Second-class cultural relics
30 cm in height

黄釉男立俑

唐代
陶器
二级文物
高25.5厘米

Yellow-glazed standing male figure
Tang Dynasty
Pottery
Second-class cultural relics
25.5 cm in height

绿釉男立俑

唐代 Green-glazed standing male figure

陶器 Tang Dynasty

二级文物 Pottery

高28厘米 Second-class cultural relics

28 cm in height

三彩文官俑

唐代

陶器

二级文物

纵 17 厘米　横 12.5 厘米

高 67 厘米

Tri-colored figure of civil official

Tang Dynasty

Pottery

Second-class cultural relics

17 cm in length　12.5 cm in width

67 cm in height

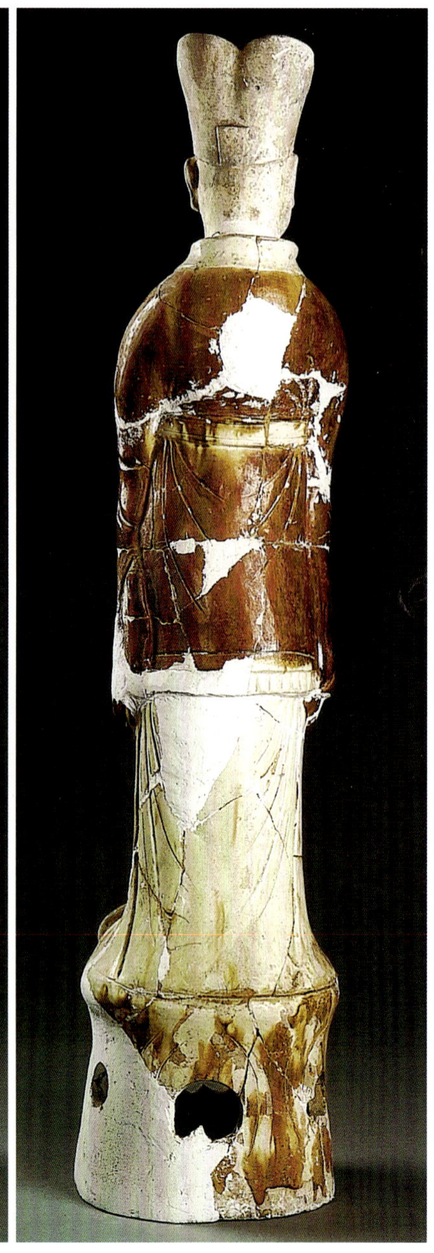

三彩文官俑

唐代	Tri-colored figure of civil official
陶器	Tang Dynasty
二级文物	Pottery
	Second-class cultural relics
纵 26 厘米　横 22 厘米	26 cm in length　22 cm in width
高 112 厘米	112 cm in height

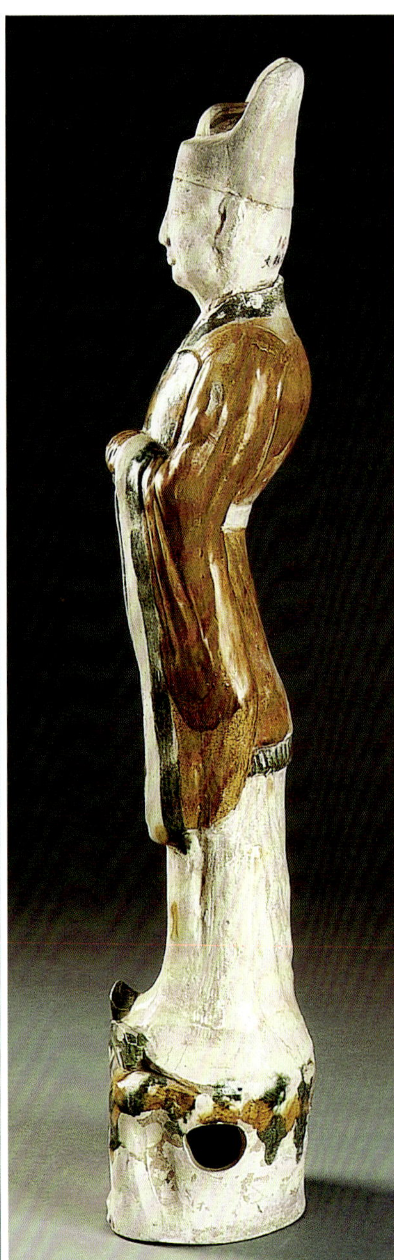

三彩文官俑

唐代 Tri-colored figure of civil official

陶器 Tang Dynasty

二级文物 Pottery

Second-class cultural relics

高77厘米 77 cm in height

三彩文吏俑

唐代
陶器
二级文物
高74厘米

Tri-colored figure of guvernment clerk
Tang Dynasty
Pottery
Second-class cultural relics
74 cm in height

三彩武俑

唐代	Tri-colored warrior figure
陶器	Tang Dynasty
二级文物	Pottery
	Second-class cultural relics
长17厘米　宽25.3厘米	17 cm in length　25.3 cm in width
高71厘米	71 cm in height

三彩武士俑

唐代	Tri-colored warrior figure
陶器	Tang Dynasty
二级文物	Pottery
	Second-class cultural relics
高 65.5 厘米	65.5 cm in length

三彩武士俑

唐代	Tri-colored warrior figure
陶器	Tang Dynasty
二级文物	Pottery
高65厘米	Second-class cultural relics
	65 cm in height

三彩胡俑

唐代	Tri-colored figure of the non-Han nationalities
陶器	Tang Dynasty
二级文物	Pottery
高31.2厘米	Second-class cultural relics
	31.2 cm in height

绿釉男俑
唐代
陶器
二级文物
高28.8厘米

Green-glazed male figure
Tang Dynasty
Pottery
Second-class cultural relics
28.8 cm in height

胡商俑

唐代
陶器
一级文物
高23.5厘米

Businessman figure of the non–Han nationalities
Tang Dynasty
Pottery
First–class cultural relics
23.5 cm in height

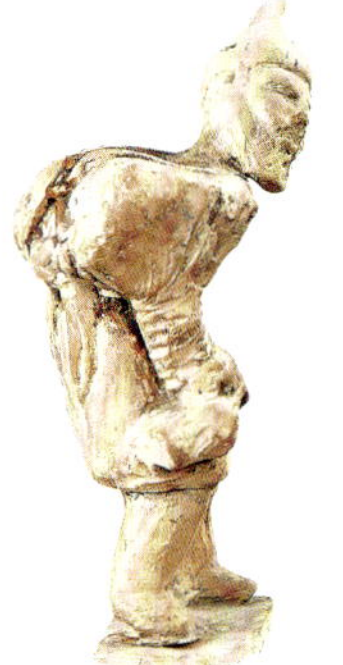

三彩武士俑
唐代
陶器
二级文物
最宽33.5厘米 厚16.5厘米
高88厘米

Tri-colored warrior figure
Tang Dynasty
Pottery
Second-class cultural relics
33.5 cm in max width 16.5 cm in thickness
88 cm in height

三彩武士俑

唐代
陶器
二级文物
高67.5厘米

Tri-colored warrior figure
Tang Dynasty
Pottery
Second-class cultural relics
67.5 cm in height

三彩文官俑

陶器 Tri-colored figure of civil official

二级文物 Pottery

通高79厘米 Second-class cultural relics

79 cm in height

三彩文官俑

陶器

二级文物

纵 11.3 厘米　横 8 厘米

高 41 厘米

Tri-colored figure of civil official

Pottery

Second-class cultural relics

11.3 cm in length　8 cm in width

41 cm in height

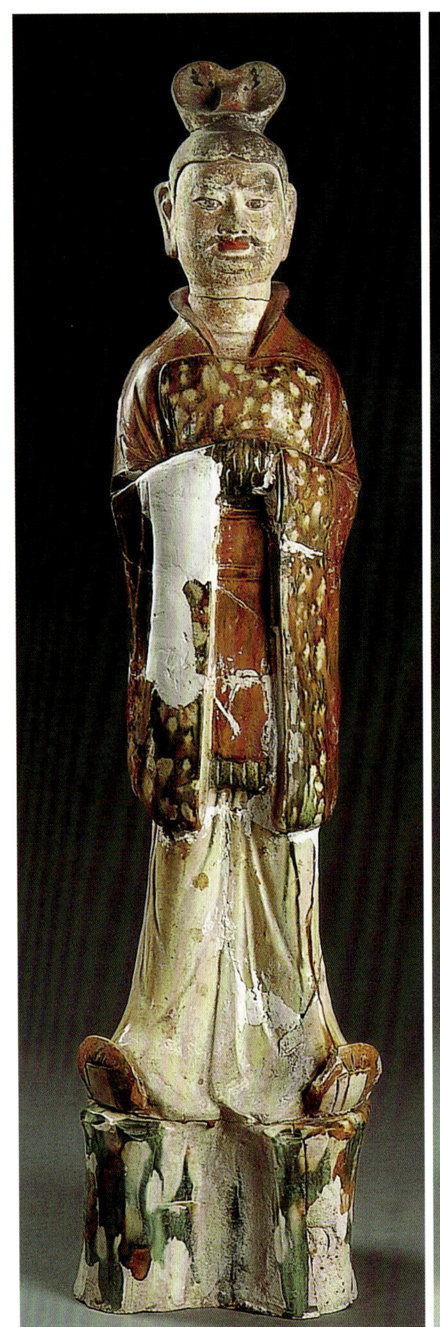

三彩文吏俑

唐代	Tri-colored figure of government clerk
陶器	Tang Dynasty
二级文物	Pottery
纵 23 厘米　横 20 厘米	Second-class cultural relics
高 95 厘米	23 cm in length 20 cm in width
	95 cm in height

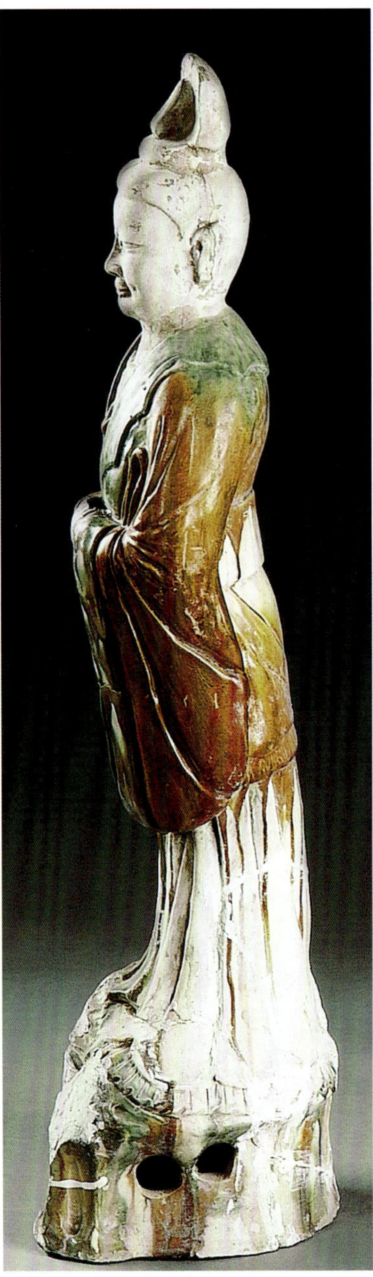

三彩文吏俑
唐代
陶器
二级文物
纵 21 厘米　横 20 厘米
高 83 厘米

Tri-colored figure of government clerk
Tang Dynasty
Pottery
Second-class cultural relics
21 cm in length　20 cm in width
83 cm in height

三彩武士俑

唐代	Tri-colored warrior figure
陶器	Tang Dynasty
二级文物	Pottery
高41.3厘米	Second-class cultural relics
	41.3 cm in height

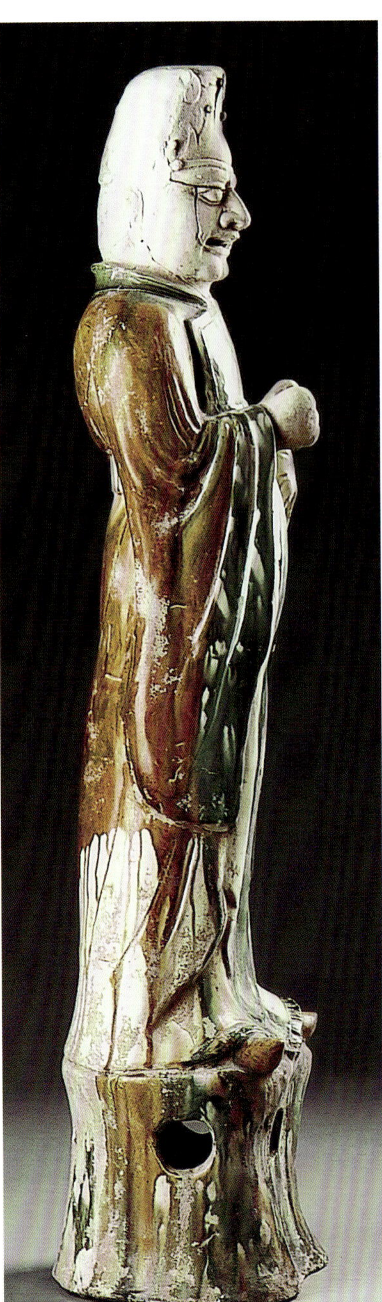

三彩文官俑
唐代
陶器
二级文物
宽 22.5 厘米　高 91 厘米

Tri-colored figure of civil official
Tang Dynasty
Pottery
Second-class cultural relics
22.5 cm in width　91 cm in height

三彩文官俑

唐代	Tri-colored figure of civil ofticial
陶器	Tang Dynasty
二级文物	Pottery
宽 22.5 厘米　高 91 厘米	Second-class cultural relics
	22.5 cm in width　91 cm in height

三彩武士俑

唐代	Tri-colored warrior figure
陶器	Tang Dynasty
	Pottery
二级文物	Second-class cultural relics
高 44 厘米	44 cm in height

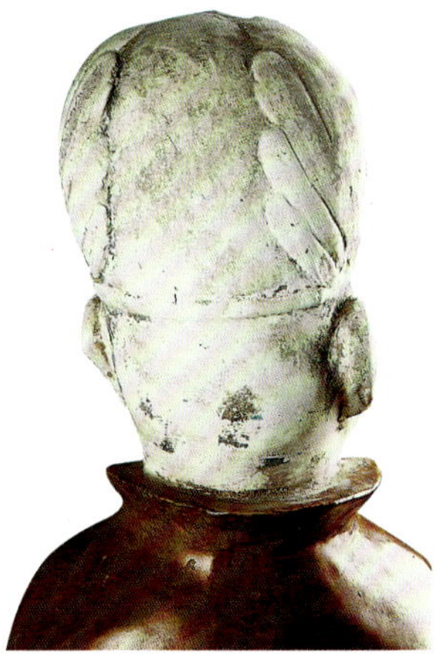

三彩文吏俑

唐代 Tri-colored figure of government clerk

陶器 Tang Dynasty

Pottery

二级文物 Second-class cultural relics

高71厘米 71 cm in height

三彩武士俑

唐代	Tri-colored warrior figure
陶器	Tang Dynasty
二级文物	Pottery
高44厘米	Second-class cultural relics
	44 cm in height

三彩文吏俑

陶器

二级文物

高70厘米

Tri-colored figure of govemment clerk

Pottery

Second-class cultural relics

70 cm in height

三彩文吏俑

陶器 | Tri-colored figure of government clerk

二级文物 | Pottery

上部最宽17厘米 | Second-class cultural relics

高72.5厘米 | 17 cm in width

72.5 cm in height

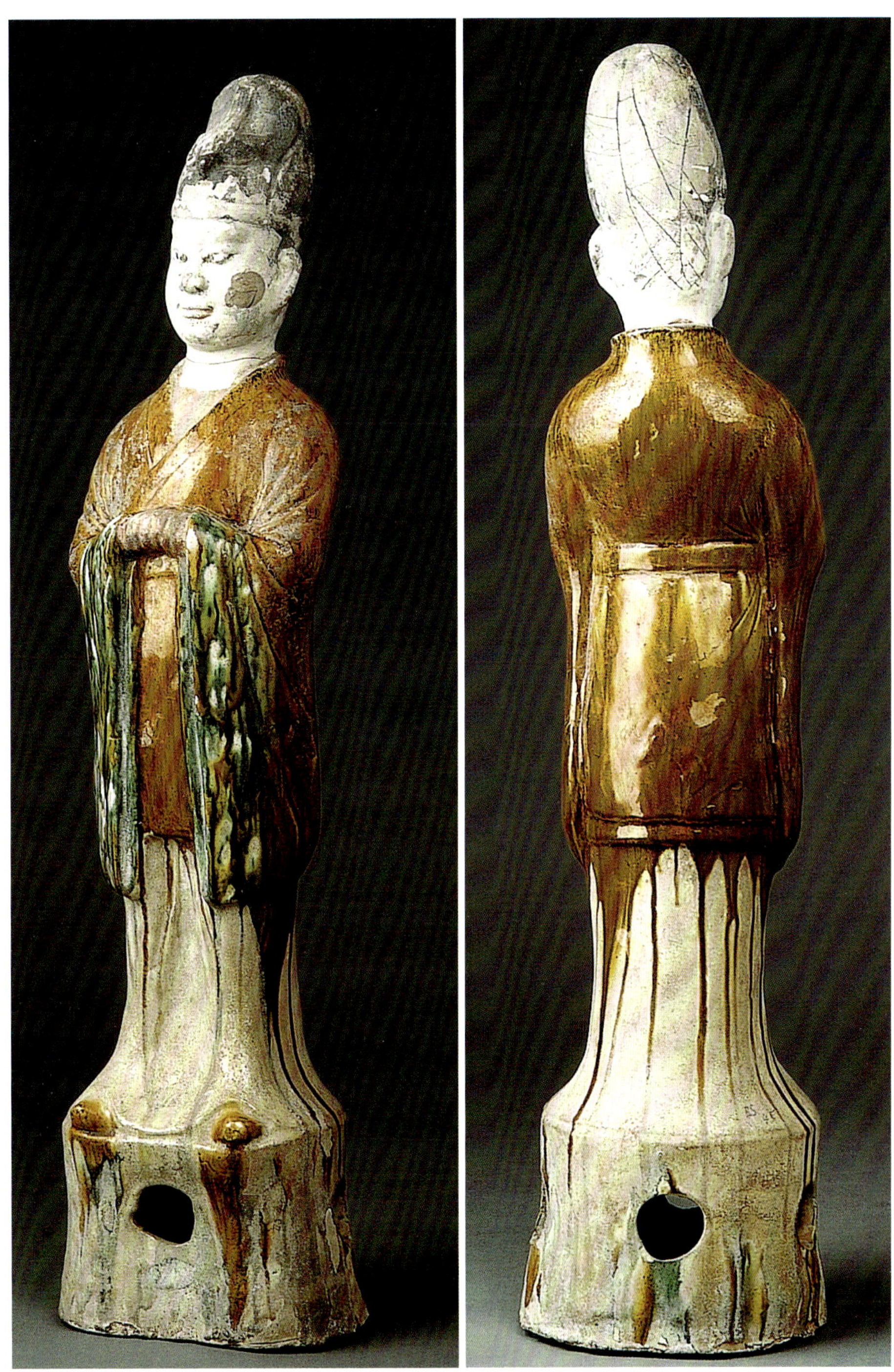

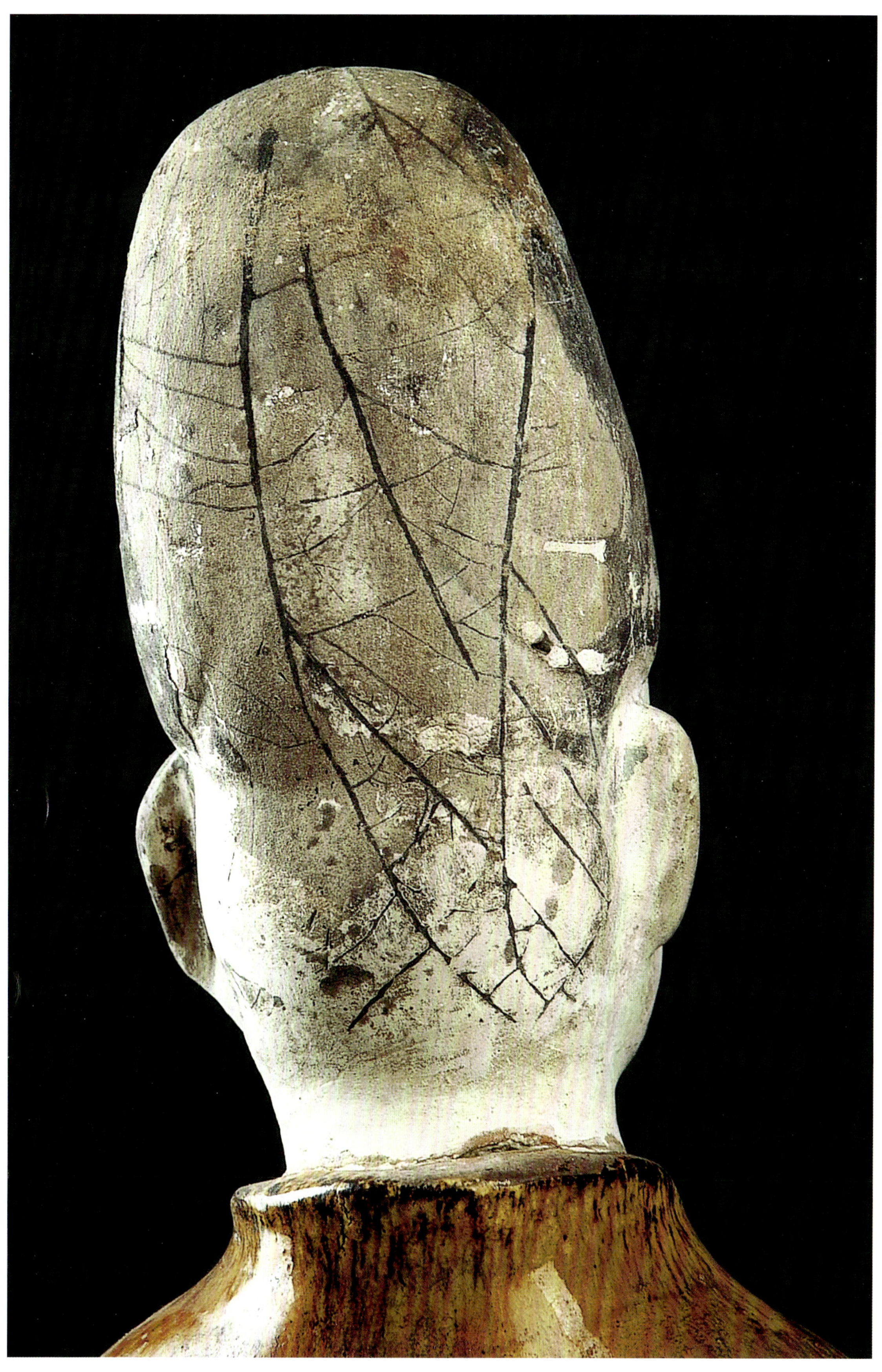

三彩武俑

唐代　Tri-colored warrior figure

陶器　Tang Dynasty

二级文物　Pottery

Second-class cultural relics

纵18.5厘米　横7.3厘米　18.5 cm in length　7.3 cm in width

高43厘米　43 cm in height

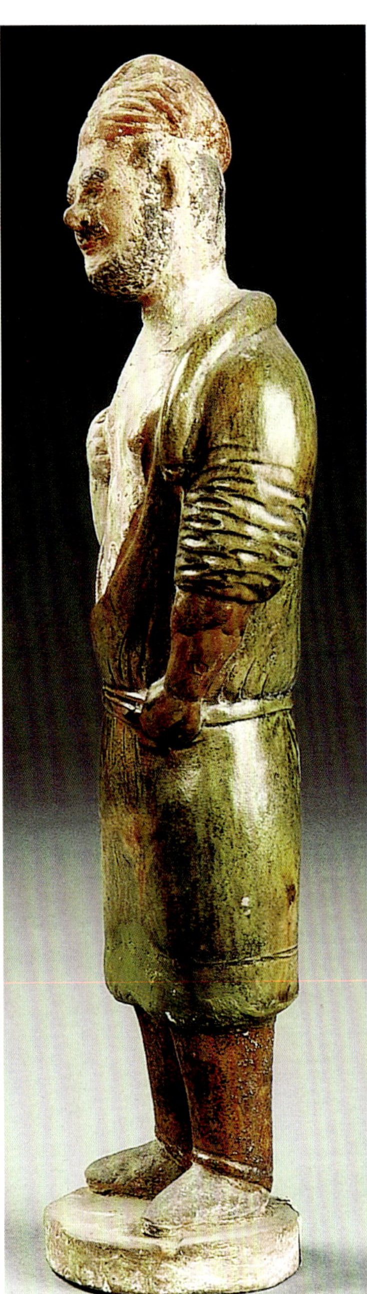

绿釉男胡俑

唐代
陶器
一级文物
高30厘米

Green-glazed male figure of the non-Han nationalities
Tang Dynasty
Pottery
First-class cultural relics
30 cm in height

黄釉绿领男胡俑

陶器

二级文物

高22.8厘米

Yellow-glazed male figure of the non-Han nationalities with green collar

Pottery

Second-class cultural relics

22.8 cm in height

三彩武俑

唐代 Tri-colored warrior figure

陶器 Tang Dynasty

二级文物 Pottery

Second-class cultural relics

纵 17.5 厘米　横 8 厘米　17.5 cm in length　8 cm in width

高 41 厘米　41 cm in height

三彩文官俑

唐代

陶器

二级文物

纵 11 厘米　横 8.8 厘米

高 41.5 厘米

Tri-colored figure of civil official

Tang Dynasty

Pottery

Second-class cultural relics

11 cm in length　8.8 cm in width

41.5 cm in height

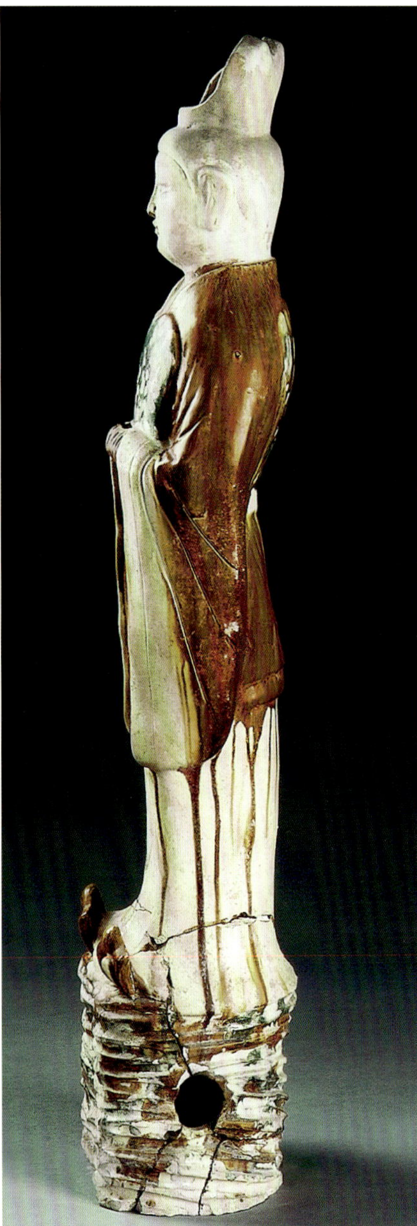
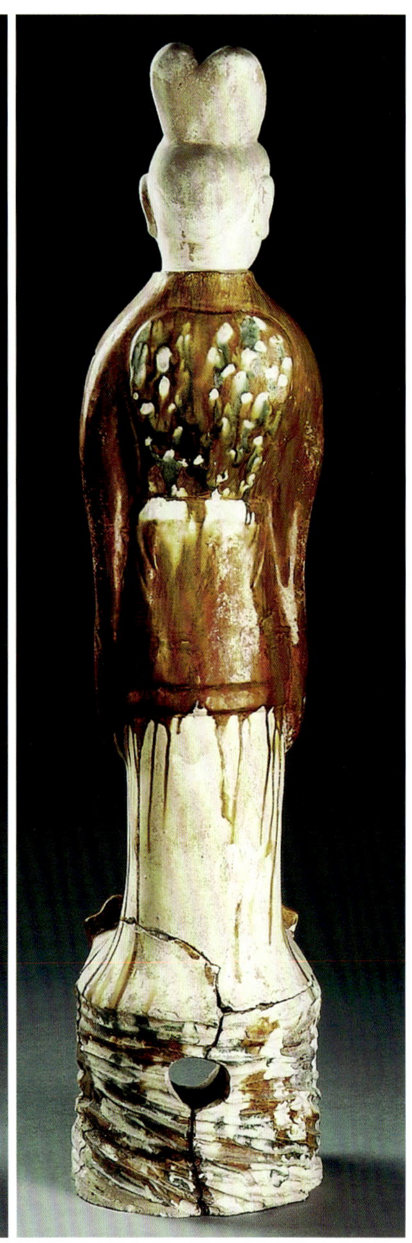

三彩文吏俑

唐代	Tri-colored figure of government clerk
陶器	Tang Dynasty
二级文物	Pottery
纵 21 厘米　横 20 厘米	Second-class cultural relics
高 83 厘米	21 cm in length　20 cm in width
	83 cm in height

三彩文官俑

唐代
陶器
二级文物
纵 19 厘米　横 18.5 厘米
高 85.5 厘米

Tri-colored figure of civil official
Tang Dynasty
Pottery
Second-class cultural relics
19 cm in length　18.5 cm in width
85.5 cm in height

三彩文吏俑

唐代　Tri-colored figure of government clerk
陶器　Tang Dynasty
二级文物　Pottery
Second-class cultural relics
纵 23 厘米　横 21 厘米　23 cm in length　21 cm in width
高 100 厘米　100 cm in height

三彩文官俑

陶器
二级文物
纵17.2厘米　横13厘米
高68厘米

Tri-colored figure of civil official
Pottery
Second-class cultural relics
17.2 cm in length　13 cm in width
68 cm in height

三彩文官俑

唐代	Tri-colored figure of civil official
陶器	Tang Dynasty
二级文物	Pottery
纵 12.5 厘米　横 8.5 厘米	Second-class cultural relics
高 42.5 厘米	12.5 cm in length　8.5 cm in width
	42.5 cm in height

三彩黄釉立领男胡俑

陶器

二级文物

高24.3厘米

Tri-colored yellow-glazed male figure of the non-Han nationalities with straight collar

Pottery

Second-class cultural relics

24.3 cm in height

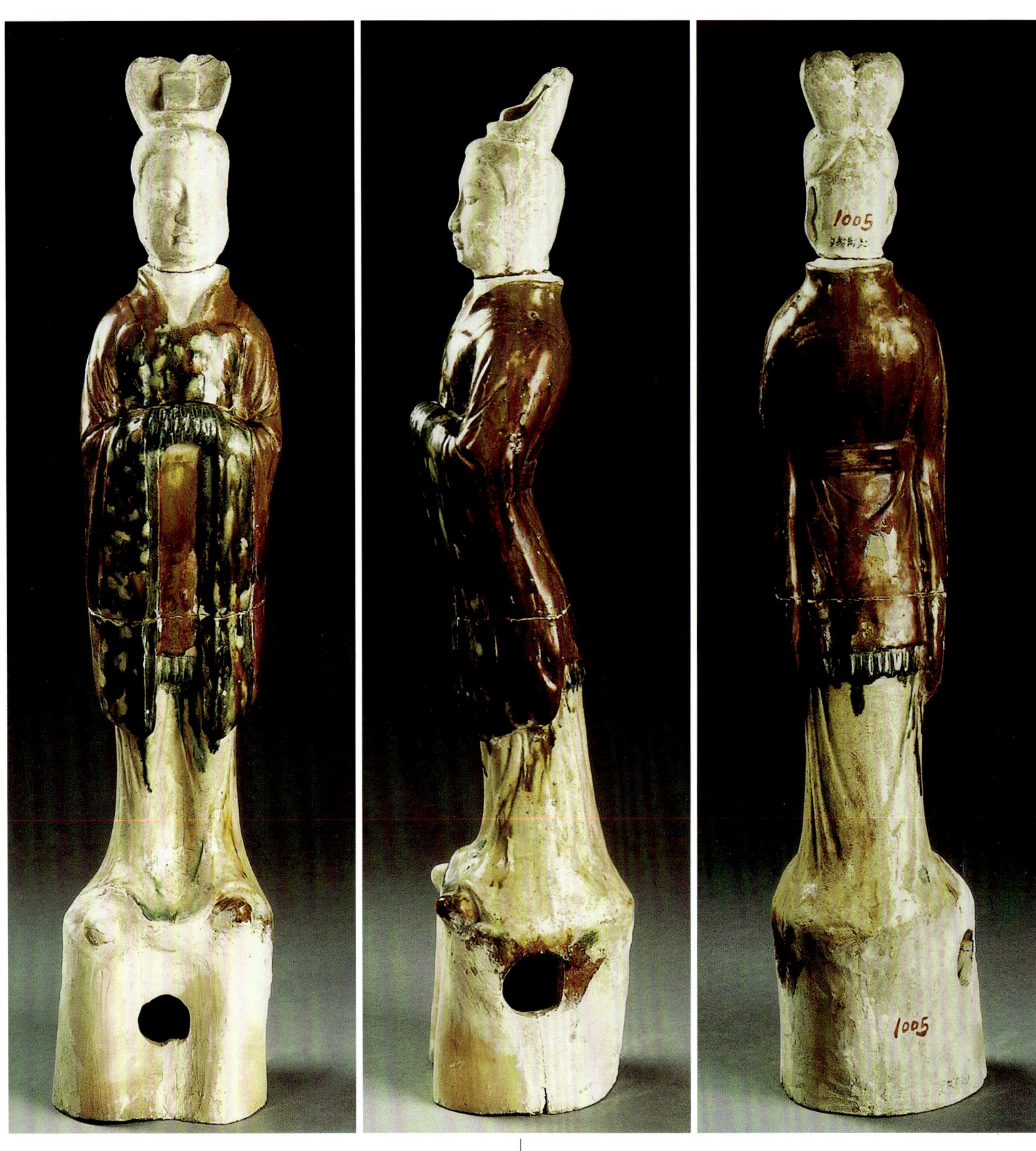

三彩文官俑

唐代
陶器
二级文物
纵 17.5 厘米　横 15.5 厘米
高 76 厘米

Tri-colored figure of civil official
Tang Dynasty
Pottery
Second-class cultural relics
17.5 cm in length　15.5 cm in width
76 cm in height

三彩文官俑

唐代	Tri-colored figure of civil official
陶器	Tang Dynasty
二级文物	Pottery
纵 17 厘米　横 16 厘米	Second-class cultural relics
高 75 厘米	17 cm in length　16 cm in width
	75 cm in height

三彩文官俑	
唐代	Tri-colored figure of civil official
陶器	Tang Dynasty
	Pottery
二级文物	Second-class cultural relics
纵 18 厘米　横 13 厘米	18 cm in length　13 cm in width
高 70.5 厘米	70.5 cm in height

三彩文官俑

唐代
陶器
二级文物
纵24厘米　横18.5厘米
高92厘米

Tri-colored figure of civil official
Tang Dynasty
Pottery
Second-class cultural relics
24 cm in length　18.5 cm in width
92 cm in height

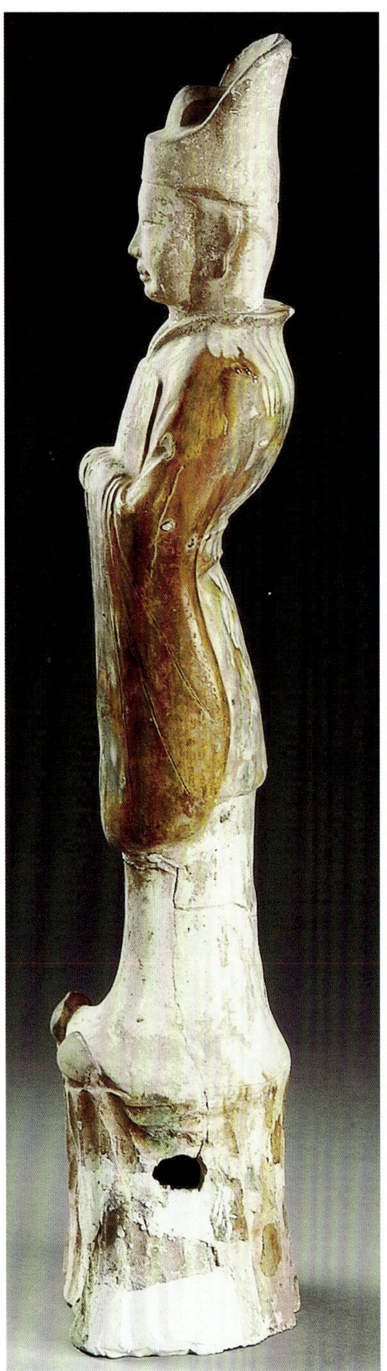

三彩文官俑

唐代	Tri-colored figure of civil official
陶器	Tang Dynasty
二级文物	Pottery
纵16.5厘米　横14.5厘米	Second-class cultural relics
高78厘米	16.5 cm in length　14.5 cm in width
	78 cm in height

三彩男伶俑

唐代	Tri-colored male actor figure
陶器	Tang Dynasty
二级文物	Pottery
高36厘米	Second-class cultural relics
	36 cm in height

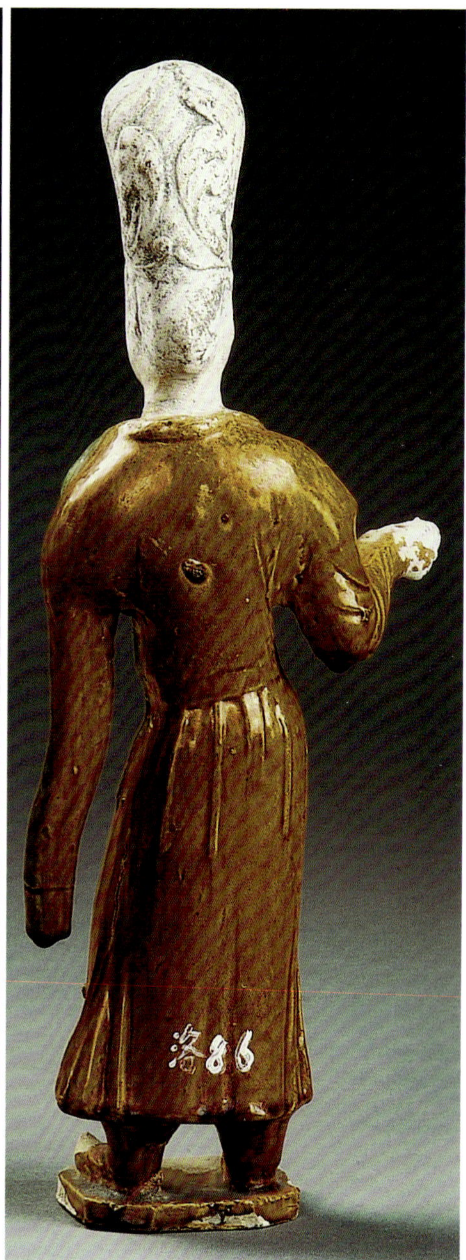

三彩黄绿釉伶俑

陶器

二级文物

高37厘米　最宽14.5厘米

厚7厘米

Tri-colored yellow-and-green glazed performer figure

Pottery

Second-class cultural relics

37 cm in height　14.5 cm in width

7 cm in thickness

人俑

女俑

三彩拱手女俑
唐代
陶器
一级文物
高33厘米　宽11厘米

Tri-colored cupping-hands female figure
Tang Dynasty
Pottery
First-class cultural relics
33 cm in height　11 cm in width

三彩丫髻女俑

唐代	Tri-colored female figure with double-bun
陶器	Tang Dynasty
二级文物	Pottery
高35.2厘米	Second-class cultural relics
宽11.3厘米　厚11.2厘米	35.2 cm in height
	11.3 cm in width　11.2 cm in thickness

单刀髻女俑

唐代
陶器
二级文物
高 39.9 厘米

Tri-colored female figure with blade-shaped bun
Tang Dynasty
Pottery
Second-class cultural relics
39.9 cm in height

黄釉女立俑

唐代　Tri-colored yellow-glazed standing female figure

陶器　Tang Dynasty

二级文物　Pottery

高23.3厘米　Second-class cultural relics

23.3 cm in height

三彩螺髻女侍俑

唐代
陶器
二级文物

Tri-colored figure of maid with spiral bun
Tang Dynasty
Pottery
Second-class cultural relics

三彩红釉螺髻女侍俑

唐代
陶器
二级文物
高27.5厘米

Tri-colored red-glazed figure of maid with spiral bun
Tang Dynasty
Pottery
Second-class cultural relics
27.5 cm in height

三彩螺髻女侍俑

唐代
陶器
二级文物
高27.5厘米

Tri-colored figure of maid with spiral bun
Tang Dynasty
Pottery
Second-class cultural relics
27.5 cm in height

三彩宝髻垂练髻女俑

唐代
陶器
二级文物
宽11厘米　厚9.5厘米
高32厘米

Tri-colored female figure with a bun and two coils
Tang Dynasty
Pottery
Second-class cultural relics
11 cm in width　9.5 cm in thickness
32 cm in height

三彩垂髻女俑

陶器
二级文物
高19.2厘米

Tri-colored female figure with a coil
Pottery
Second-class cultural relics
19.2 cm in height

三彩半翻髻女俑

陶器	Tri-colored female figure with folded bun
二级文物	Pottery
高25厘米	Second-class cultural relics
	25 cm in height

三彩螺髻女侍俑
陶器
二级文物
高25.3厘米

Tri-colored figure of maid with spiral bun
Pottery
Second-class cultural relics
25.3 cm in height

三彩垂髻女俑

陶器
二级文物
高 18.5 厘米

Tri-colored female figure with a coil
Pottery
Second-class cultural relics
18.5 cm in height

三彩双高髻女俑

唐代

陶器

二级文物

Tri-colored female figure with double buns

Tang Dynasty

Pottery

Second-class cultural relics

三彩螺髻女侍俑

唐代	Tri-colored figure of maid with spiral bun
陶器	Tang Dynasty
二级文物	Pottery
高27厘米	Second-class cultural relics
	27 cm in height

三彩女侍俑

唐代
陶器
二级文物
高33厘米

Tri-colored figure of maid
Tang Dynasty
Pottery
Second-class cultural relics
33 cm in height

三彩女侍俑

唐代 Tri-colored figure of maid

陶器 Tang Dynasty

二级文物 Pottery

Second-class cultural relics

高33厘米 33 cm in height

三彩女立俑	
唐代	Tri-colored standing female figure
陶器	Tang Dynasty
二级文物	Pottery
高33.3厘米	Second-class cultural relics
	33.3 cm in height

三彩单刀髻女俑

陶器

二级文物

纵 9 厘米　横 9 厘米

高 39 厘米

Tri-colored female figure with blade-shaped bun

Pottery

Second-class cultural relics

9 cm in length　9 cm in width

39 cm in height

三彩鹦鹉髻女俑

陶器

一级文物

宽10厘米　厚10.5厘米

高33.4厘米

Tri-colored female figure with parrot-shaped bun

Pottery

First-class cultural relics

10 cm in width　10.5 cm in thickness

33.4 cm in height

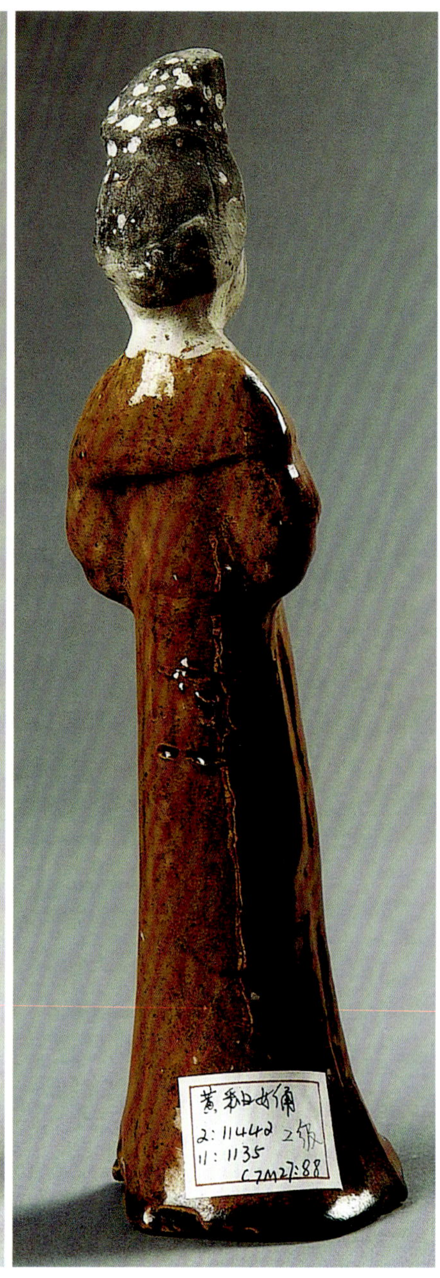

三彩螺髻女侍俑

唐代
陶器
二级文物
高36厘米

Tri-colored figure of maid with spiral bun
Tang Dynasty
Pottery
Second-class cultural relics
36 cm in height

三彩女坐俑

陶器

一级文物

高26厘米　宽10.4厘米

厚10.6厘米

Tri-colored sitting female figure

Pottery

First-class cultural relics

26 cm in height　10.4 cm in width

10.6 cm in thickness

三彩螺髻女侍俑

唐代 | Tri-colored figure of maid with spiral bun
陶器 | Tang Dynasty
二级文物 | Pottery
高28厘米 | Second-class cultural relics
28 cm in height

人俑

人(动)物俑

三彩骑马击鼓男俑

唐代
陶器
一级文物
高38厘米　长35.5厘米

Tri-colored horse- riding and drum-beating male figure
Tang Dynasty
Pottery
First-class cultural relics
38 cm in height　35.5 cm in length

三彩牵马男俑
陶器
二级文物
高45厘米

Tri-colored horse-leading male figure
Pottery
Second-class cultural relics
45 cm in height

三彩牵马男俑

陶器
二级文物
高43厘米

Tri-colored horse-leading male figure
Pottery
Second-class cultural relics
43 cm in height

三彩骑马女俑

唐代

陶器

二级文物

长33厘米　高38.4厘米

Tri-colored horse- riding female figure

Tang Dynasty

Pottery

Second-class cultural relics

33 cm in length　38.4 cm in height

三彩骑马女俑

陶器

二级文物

纵34厘米　高38.5厘米

Tri-colored horse-riding female figure

Pottery

Second-class cultural relics

34 cm in length　38.5 cm in height

三彩牵驼俑

陶器
二级文物
高 60 厘米

Tri-colored camel-leading figure
Pottery
Second-class cultural relics
60 cm in height

三彩骑马男俑

陶器	Tri-colored horse-riding male figure
二级文物	Pottery
通高39.7厘米	Second-class cultural relics
通长36厘米	39.7 cm in height
	36 cm in length

三彩骑马男俑

唐代

陶器

二级文物

长35厘米　高42厘米

Tri-colored horse- riding male figure

Tang Dynasty

Pottery

Secind-class cultural relics

35 cm in length　42 cm in height

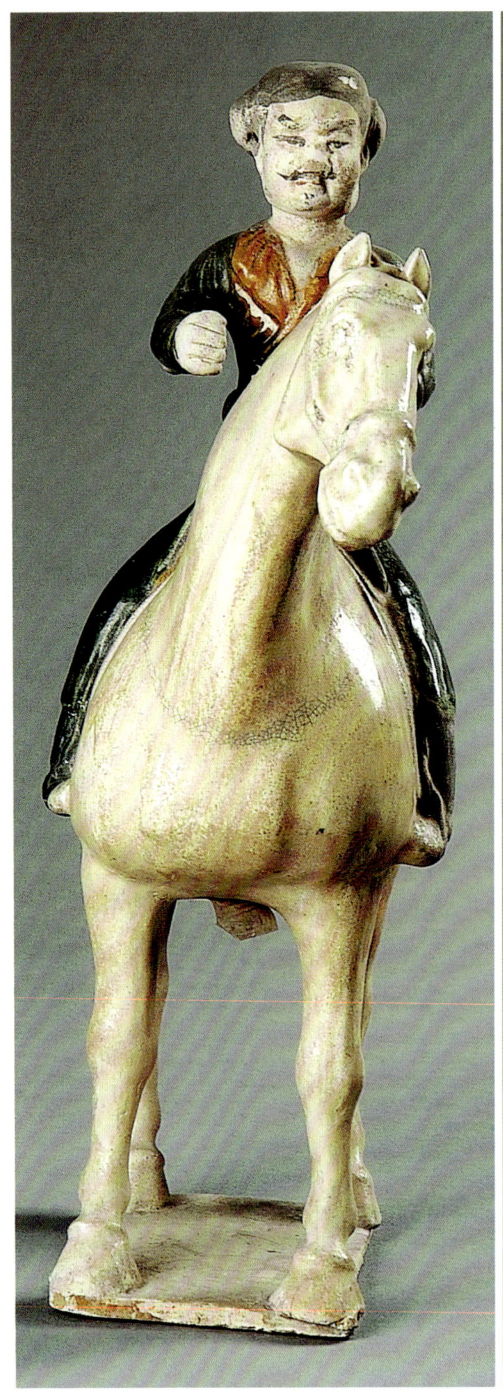

三彩骑马男俑

陶器

二级文物

通高 38 厘米　通长 41 厘米

Tri-colored horse-riding male figure

Pottery

Second-class cultural reliCs

38 cm in height　41 cm in length

三彩牵马俑

陶器

一级文物

高 66 厘米

Tri-colored horse-leading figure

Pottery

First-class cultural relics

66 cm in height

三彩胡人骑马俑

陶器

二级文物

长 38.7 厘米　宽 12.8 厘米

高 41 厘米

Tri-colored horse-riding figure of the non-Han nationaliies

Pottery

Second-class cultural relics

38.7 cm in length　12.8 cm in width

41 cm in height

三彩束发男胡人牵马俑

陶器
一级文物
宽 20 厘米　纵 22 厘米
高 62 厘米

Tri-colored hair-tied horse-lead ing male figure of the non-Han nationaliies
Pottery
First-class cultural relics
20 cm in width　22 cm in length
62 cm in height

三彩高胡帽男牵马俑

陶器
一级文物
宽22.5厘米　厚14.5厘米
高67.5厘米

Tri-colored horse-leading male figure with Hu's hat
Pottery
First-class cultural relics
22.5 cm in width　14.5 cm in thickness
67.5 cm in height

三彩牵马俑

陶器
一级文物
高66厘米

Tri-colored horse-leading figure
Pottery
First-class cultural relics
66 cm in height

三彩骑马男俑

陶器

二级文物

长 36.4 厘米　高 41 厘米

Tri-colored horse-riding male figure

Pottery

Second-class cultural relics

36.4 cm in length　41 cm in height

三彩牵驼男俑

唐代 | Tri-colored camel-rleading male figure
陶器 | Tang Dynasty
二级文物 | Pottery
高 49 厘米 | Second-class cultural relics
49 cm in height

三彩骑马男俑

陶器 | Tri-colored horse-riding male figure
二级文物 | Pottery
横 34 厘米 | Second-class cultural relics
高 41.4 厘米 | 34 cm in width
41.4 cm in height

三彩骑马男俑

陶器
二级文物
通高39厘米
通长36厘米

Tri-colored horse-riding male figure
Pottery
Second-class cultural relics
39 cm in height
36 cm in length

三彩骑马女俑	
陶器	Tri-colored horse-riding female figure
二级文物	Pottery
通高 41.9 厘米	Second-class cultural relics
通长 40 厘米	41.9 cm in height
	40 cm in length

三彩骑马男俑

唐代
陶器
二级文物
长35.5厘米
高41.4厘米

Tri-colored horse-riding male figure
Tang Dynasty
Pottery
Second-class cultural relics
35.5 cm in length
41.4 cm in height

三彩牵马俑

唐代	Tri-colored horse-leading figure
陶器	Tang Dynasty
	Pottery
二级文物	Second-class cultural relics
高46厘米	46 cm in height

三彩骑马女俑

陶器

二级文物

长 33.7 厘米　厚 11 厘米

高 41 厘米

Tri-colored horse-riding female figure

Pottery

Second-class cultural relics

33.7 cm in length　11 cm in thickness

41 cm in height

三彩牵马俑

唐代	Tri-colored horse-leading figure
陶器	Tang Dynasty
二级文物	Pottery
纵 16 厘米　横 12 厘米	Second-class cultural relics
高 42.5 厘米	16 cm in length　12 cm in width
	42.5 cm in height

三彩牵马俑

唐代
陶器
二级文物
纵16厘米　横10厘米
高43.5厘米

Tri-colored horse-leading figure
Tang Dynasty
Pottery
Second-class cultural relics
16 cm in length　10 cm in width
43.5 cm in height

黄釉牵马俑

唐代	Yellow-glazed horse-leading figure
陶器	Tang Dynasty
二级文物	Pottery
	Second-class cultural relics
纵 18 厘米　横 11 厘米	18 cm in length　11 cm in width
高 43 厘米	43 cm in height

三彩牵驼俑

唐代	Tri-colored camel-leading figure
陶器	Tang Dynasty
一级文物	Pottery
高 62 厘米	First-class cultural relics
	62 cm in height

白釉牵马俑

唐代	Tri-colored white -glazed horse-leading figure
陶器	Tang Dynasty
二级文物	Pottery
	Second-class cultural relis
纵 21 厘米　横 15.5 厘米	21 cm in length　15.5 cm in width
高 62 厘米	62 cm in height

三彩牵马俑

唐代
陶器
二级文物
纵 13.5 厘米　横 11 厘米
高 33 厘米

Tri-colored horse-leading figure
Tang Dynasty
Pottery
Second-class cultural relics
13.5 cm in length　11 cm in width
33 cm in height

三彩牵驼俑

唐代	Tri-colored camel-leading figure
陶器	Tang Dynasty
一级文物	Pottery
宽 21.5 厘米	First-class cultural relics
高 59 厘米	21.5 cm in width
	59 cm in height

三彩牵马俑
唐代
陶器
二级文物
宽22.5厘米　高91厘米

Tri-colored horse-leading figure
Tang Dynasty
Pottery
Second-class cultural relics
22.5 cm in width　91 cm in height

三彩幞帽男牵马俑

陶器

一级文物

宽 22.5 厘米　纵 18 厘米

高 61.5 厘米

Tri-colored horse-leading male figure with felt hat

Pottery

First-class cultural relics

22.5 cm in width　18 cm in length

61.5 cm in height

三彩幞帽骑马男胡俑

陶器

二级文物

长36.5厘米　厚15.3厘米

高42.2厘米

Tri-colored horse-riding male figure of the non-Han nationalities with felt hat

Pottery

Second-class cultural relics

36.5 cm in length　15.7 cm in thickness

42.2 cm in height

三彩后堕髻牵马俑

陶器
二级文物
厚19.5厘米　宽21.5厘米
高58厘米

Tri-colored horse-leading figure with back coil
Pottery
Second-class cultural relics
19.5 cm in thickness　21.5 cm in width
58 cm in height

三彩褐釉牵马俑

唐代 Tri-colored brown-glazed horse-leading figure

陶器 Tang Dynasty

二级文物 Pottery

高45厘米 Second-class cultural relics

45 cm in height

三彩载人骆驼

唐代

陶器

一级文物

高 38 厘米　长 32 厘米

Tri-colored manned camel

Tang Dynasty

Pottery

First-class cultural relics

38 cm in height　32 cm in length

三彩绿釉牵驼俑

陶器
二级文物
高31.7厘米

Tri-colored green-glazed camel-leading figure
Pottery
Second-class cultural relics
31.7 cm in height

三彩黄釉牵马俑

唐代	Tri-colored yellow-glazed horse-leading figure
陶器	Tang Dynasty
二级文物	Pottery
最宽22厘米　厚14厘米	Second-class cultural relis
高14厘米	22 cm in max width　14 cm in thickness
	14 cm in height

三彩风帽骑马女俑

陶器

二级文物

长 36 厘米　宽 13.5 厘米

高 41 厘米

Tri-colored horse-riding female figure wearing hood

Pottery

Second-class cultural relics

36 cm in length　13.5 cm in width

41 cm in height

三彩牵马俑

唐代	Tri-colored horse-leading figure
陶器	Tang Dynasty
二级文物	Pottery
	Second-class cultural relics
纵15厘米　横11.5厘米	15 cm in length　11.5 cm in width
高42厘米	42 cm in height

人俑

神俑

三彩凤冠天王俑

唐代
陶器
一级文物
高113厘米

Tri-colored figure of heavenly king with phoenix-shaped crown
Tang Dynasty
Pottery
First-class cultural relics
113 cm in height

三彩鸟冠天王俑

唐代
陶器
一级文物
高111厘米

Tri-colored figure of heavenly king with bird-shaped crown
Tang Dynasty
Pottery
First-class cultural relics
111 cm in height

三彩天王俑

唐代	Tri-colored figure of heavenly king
陶器	Tang Dynasty
	Pottery
二级文物	Second-class cultural relics
纵 18 厘米　横 8.8 厘米	18 cm in length　8.8 cm in width
高 41 厘米	41 cm in height

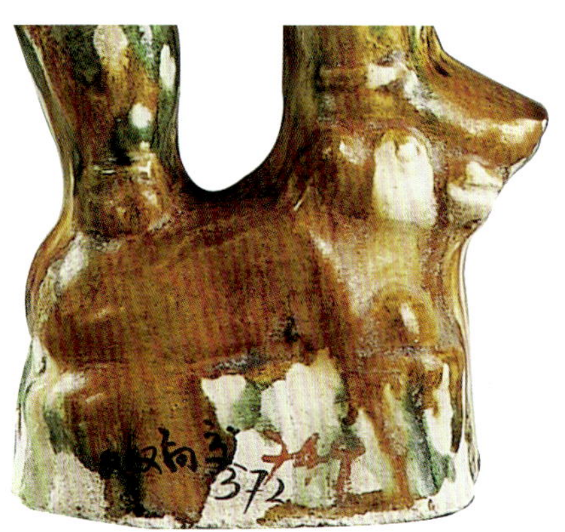

三彩天王俑

唐代

陶器

二级文物

纵 20.5 厘米　横 8.5 厘米

高 42 厘米

Tri-colored figure of heavenly king

Tang Dynasty

Pottery

Second-class cultural relics

20.5 cm in length　8.5 cm in width

42 cm in height

三彩天王俑

唐代 | Tri-colored figure of heavenly king
陶器 | Tang Dynasty
二级文物 | Pottery
纵 18 厘米　横 8.3 厘米 | Second-class cultural relics
高 43 厘米 | 18 cm in length　8.3 cm in width
43 cm in height

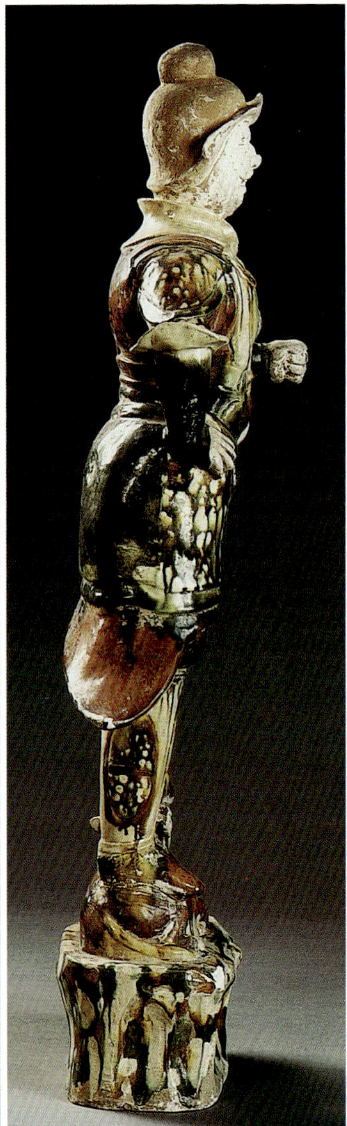

三彩天王俑

唐代	Tri-colored figure of heavenly king
陶器	Tang Dynasty
二级文物	Pottery
长 11 厘米　宽 29 厘米	Second-class cultural relics
高 80 厘米	11 cm in length　29 cm in width
	80 cm in height

三彩天王俑
陶器
一级文物
高 61 厘米

Tri-colored figure of heavenly king
Pottery
First-class cultural relics
61 cm in height

三彩天王俑

陶器 Tri-colored figure of heavenly king

一级文物 Pottery

First-class cultural relics

高62厘米 62 cm in height

三彩天王俑

唐代
陶器
二级文物
长13.8厘米　宽34厘米
高86厘米

Tri-colored figure of heavenly king
Tang Dynasty
Pottery
Second-class cultural relics
13.8 cm in length　34 cm in width
86 cm in height

三彩天王俑

唐代	Tri-colored figure of heavenly king
陶器	Tang Dynasty
	Pottery
二级文物	Second-class cultural relics
长 12 厘米　宽 35 厘米	12 cm in length　35 cm in width
高 100 厘米	100 cm in height

三彩天王俑

唐代	Tri-colored figure of heavenly king
陶器	Tang Dynasty
二级文物	Pottery
长 15 厘米　宽 36 厘米	Second-class cultural relics
高 79 厘米	15 cm in length　36 cm in width
	79 cm in height

三彩天王俑	
唐代	Tri-colored figure of heavenly king
陶器	Tang Dynasty
二级文物	Pottery
长 15 厘米　宽 27 厘米	Second-class cultural relics
高 77.5 厘米	15 cm in length　27 cm in width
	77.5 cm in height

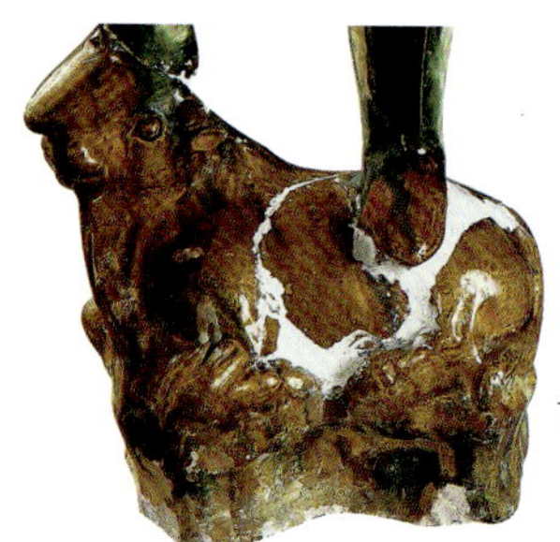

三彩天王俑

唐代
陶器
二级文物
长12.8厘米　宽46.5厘米
高78厘米

Tri-colored figure of heavenly king
Tang Dynasty
Pottery
Second-class cultural relics
12.8 cm in length　46.5 cm in width
78 cm in height

三彩鸟冠天王俑
陶器
一级文物
宽29.5厘米 厚18厘米
高64厘米

Tri-colored figure of heavenly king with bird-shaped crown
Pottery
First-class cultural relics
29.5 cm in width 18 cm in thickness
64 cm in height

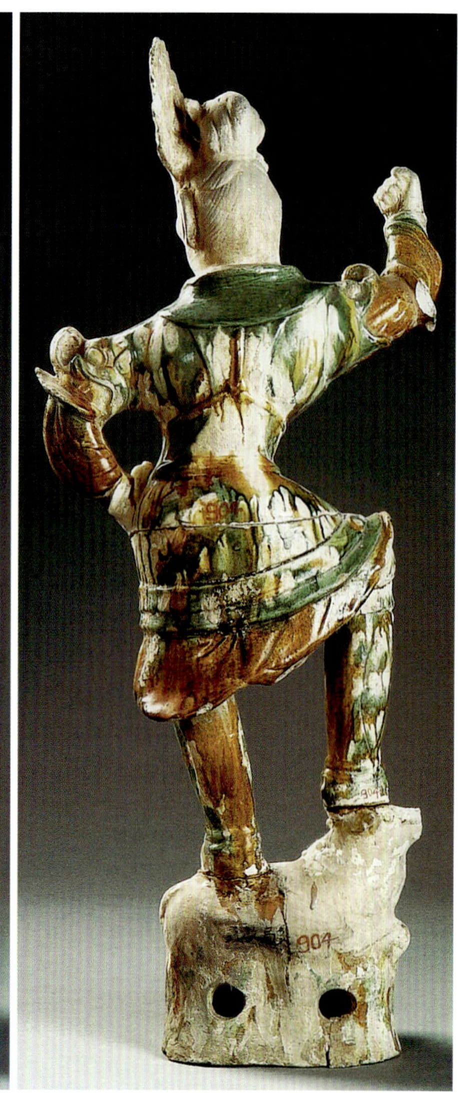

三彩天王俑

唐代
陶器
二级文物
长13厘米　宽37厘米
高85厘米

Tri-colored figure of heavenly king
Tang Dynasty
Pottery
Second-class cultural relics
13 cm in length　37 cm in width
85 cm in height

三彩天王俑
唐代
陶器
二级文物
长 15 厘米　宽 32.5 厘米
高 83.5 厘米

Tri-colored figure of heavenly king
Tang Dynasty
Pottery
Second-class cultural relics
15 cm in length　32.5 cm in width
83.5 cm in height

三彩天王俑

唐代	Tri-colored figure of heavenly king
陶器	Tang Dynasty
二级文物	Pottery
	Second-class cultural relics
长 14 厘米　宽 27 厘米	14 cm in length　27 cm in width
高 80 厘米	80 cm in height

三彩天王俑
唐代
陶器
二级文物
长 12 厘米　宽 46 厘米
高 89 厘米

Tri-colored figure of heavenly king
Tang Dynasty
Pottery
Second-class cultural relics
12 cm in length　46 cm in width
89 cm in height

三彩凤冠天王俑

陶器

一级文物

宽23.8厘米　厚17厘米

高64.5厘米

Tri-colored figure of heavenly king with phoenix-shaped crown

Pottery

First-class cultural relics

23.8 cm in width　17 cm in thickness

64.5 cm in height

三彩天王俑

唐代
陶器
二级文物
长13.8厘米　宽37厘米
高87.5厘米

Tri-colored figure of heavenly king
Tang Dynasty
Pottery
Second-class cultural relics
13.8 cm in length　37 cm in width
87.5 cm in height

三彩天王俑
唐代
陶器
二级文物
高 78 厘米

Tri-colored figure of heavenly king
Tang Dynasty
Pottery
Second-class cultural relics
78 cm in height

中国洛阳出土唐三彩全集

Collected Works on Tang Tricolor Unearthed in Luoyang, China

下

周立　高虎　编

大象出版社

三彩天王俑

唐代　Tri-colored figure of heavenly king

陶器　Tang Dynasty

二级文物　Pottery

Second-class cultural relics

长14厘米　宽35厘米　14 cm in length　35 cm in width

高89厘米　89 cm in height

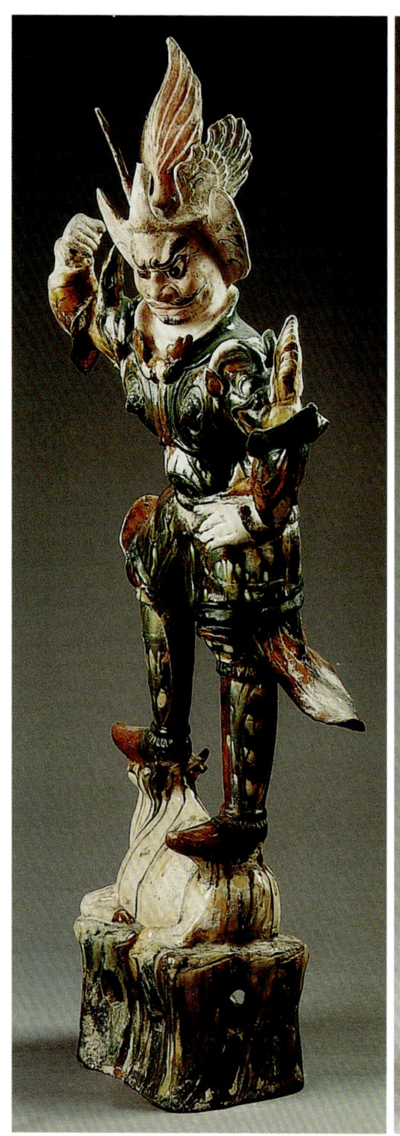

三彩天王俑
唐代
陶器
一级文物
通高113厘米

Tri-colored figure of heavenly king
Tang Dynasty
Pottery
First-class cultural relics
113 cm in height

三彩天王俑
唐代
陶器
二级文物
通高108厘米

Tri-colored figure of heavenly king
Tang Dynasty
Pottery
Second-class cultural relics
108 cm in height

三彩天王俑
陶器
二级文物
高110厘米

Tri-colored figure of heavenly king
Pottery
Second-class cultural relics
110 cm in height

三彩天王射箭俑

唐代

陶器

二级文物

通高91.5厘米

Tri-colored arrow-shooting figure of the heavenly king

Tang Dynasty

Pottery

Second-class cultural relics

91.5 cm in height

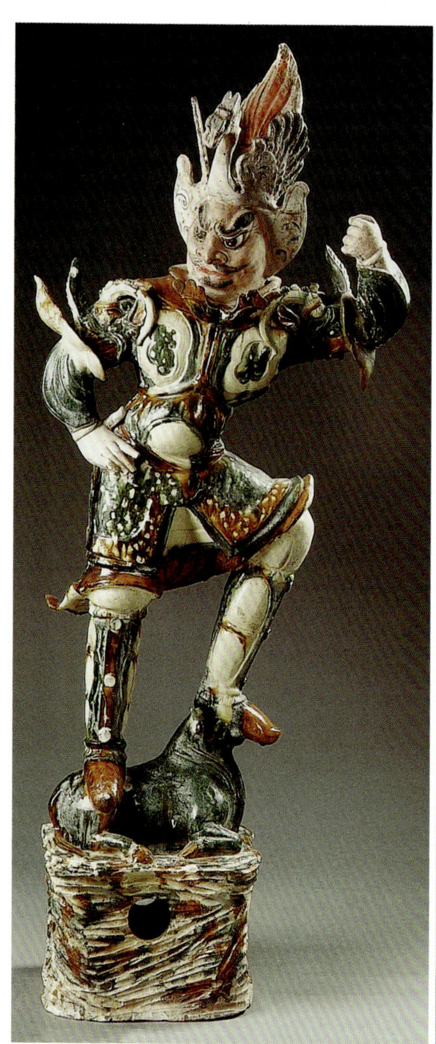

三彩天王俑
唐代
陶器
一级文物
通高113厘米

Tri-colored figure of heavenly king
Tang Dynasty
Pottery
First-class cultural relics
113 cm in height

三彩天王俑

唐代	Tri-colored figure of heavenly king
陶器	Tang Dynasty
二级文物	Pottery
	Second-class cultural relics
长 15.4 厘米　宽 25.3 厘米	15.4 cm in length　25.3 cm in width
高 81 厘米	81 cm in height

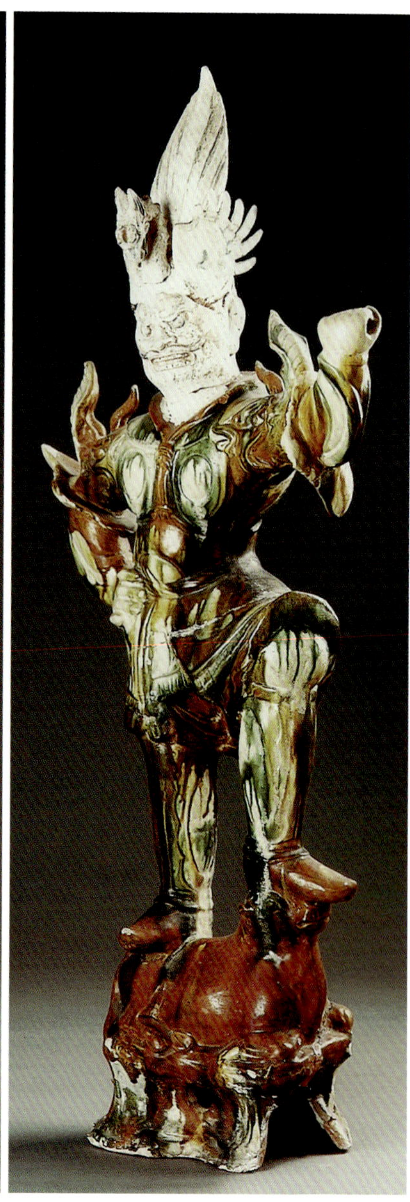

三彩天王俑

唐代
陶器
一级文物
高89厘米

Tri-colored figure of heavenly king
Tang Dynasty
Pottery
First-class cultural relics
89 cm in height

三彩天王俑

唐代
陶器
一级文物
高89.5厘米

Tri-colored figure of heavenly king
Tang Dynasty
Pottery
First-class cultural relics
89.5 cm in height

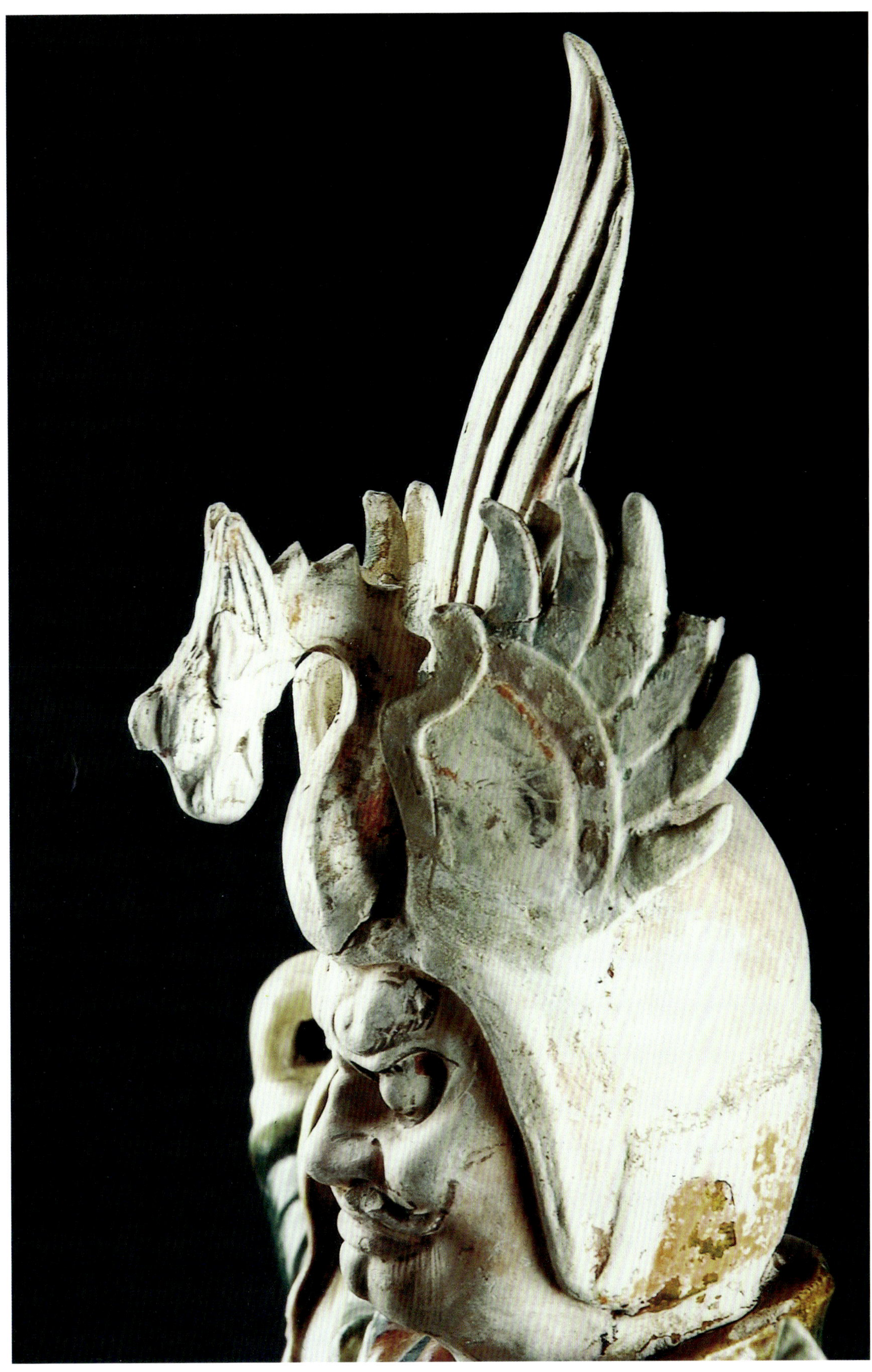

三彩天王俑

唐代 Tri-colored figure of heavenly king

陶器 Tang Dynasty

二级文物 Pottery

Second-class cultural relics

长 14 厘米　宽 38 厘米　14 cm in length　38 cm in width

高 92 厘米　92 cm in height

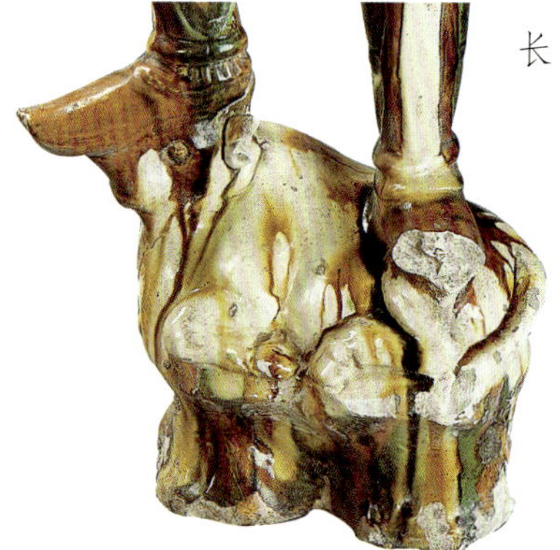

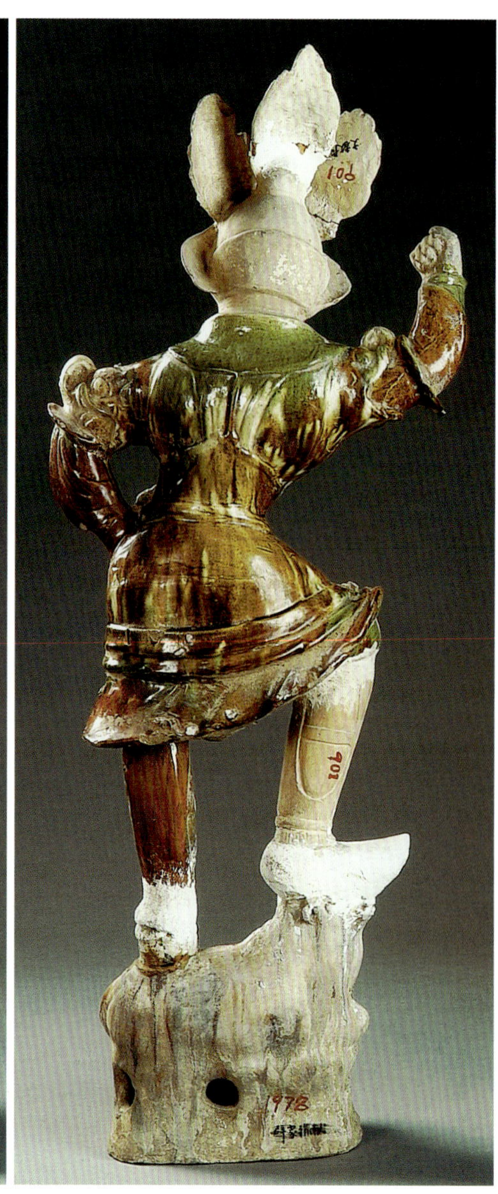

三彩天王俑

唐代 Tri-colored figure of heavenly king

陶器 Tang Dynasty

二级文物 Pottery

Second-class cultural relics

长12.8厘米 宽31.3厘米 12.8 cm in length 31.3 cm in width

高89厘米 89 cm in height

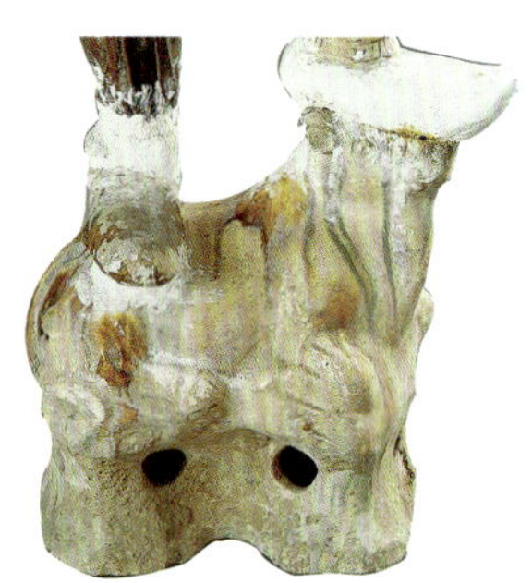

三彩天王俑

陶器
二级文物
高 41.5 厘米
最宽 41 厘米

Tri-colored figure of heavenly king
Pottery
Second-class cultural relics
41.5 cm in height
41 cm in width

三彩天王俑
陶器
二级文物
高88厘米

Tri-colored figure of heavenly king
Pottery
Second-class cultural relics
88 cm in height

三彩天王俑

唐代
陶器
二级文物
长 17 厘米　宽 42 厘米
高 113.5 厘米

Tri-colored figure of heavenly king
Tang Dynasty
Pottery
Second-class cultural relics
17 cm in length　42 cm in width
113.5 cm in height

动物俑

马俑

三彩蓝条马	
唐代	Tri-colored blue -striped horse
陶器	Tang Dynasty
一级文物	Pottery
	First-class cultural relics
高44.7厘米　长47厘米	44.7 cm in height　47 cm in length
底径22.6×16厘米	22.6 ×16 cm of base diameter

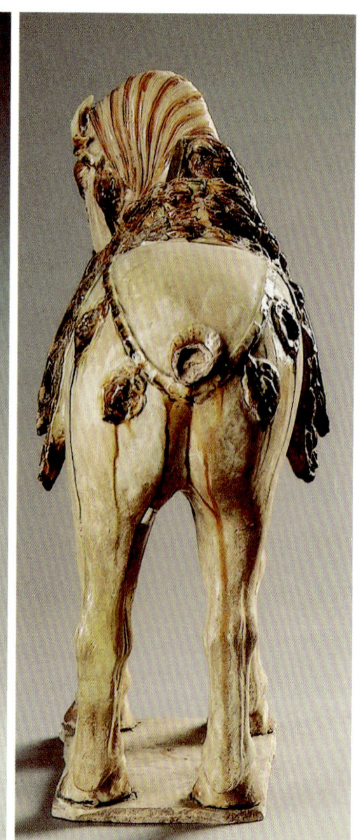

三彩白马
唐代
陶器
一级文物
高 55 厘米
长 55 厘米

Tri-colored white horse
Tang Dynasty
Pottery
First-class cultural relics
55 cm in height
55 cm in length

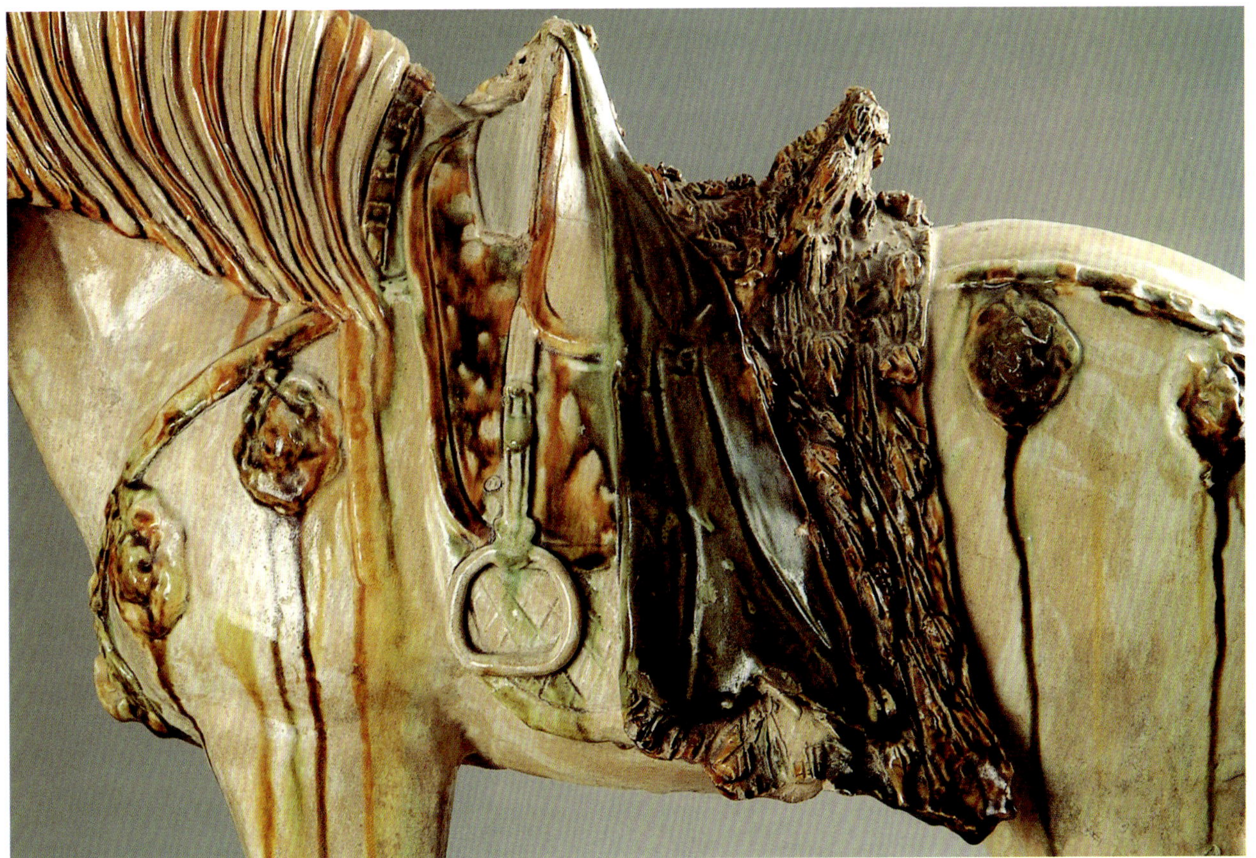

红釉白斑光背马

唐代
陶器
一级文物
高 64 厘米　长 66 厘米

Red-glazed and white-striped bare horse
Tang Dynasty
Pottery
First-class cultural relics
64 cm in height　66 cm in length

橙釉马

唐代
陶器
二级文物
长48厘米　宽14厘米
高48厘米

Orange-glazed horse
Tang Dynasty
Pottery
Second-class cultural relics
48 cm in length　14 cm in width
46 cm in height

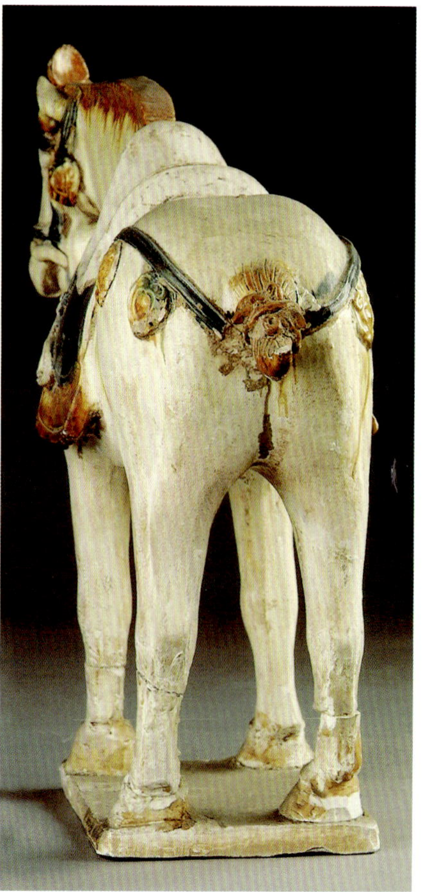

三彩白马

陶器

二级文物

高 38.5 厘米 宽 43 厘米

Tri-colored white horse

Pottery

Second-class cultural relics

38.5 cm in height 43 cm in width

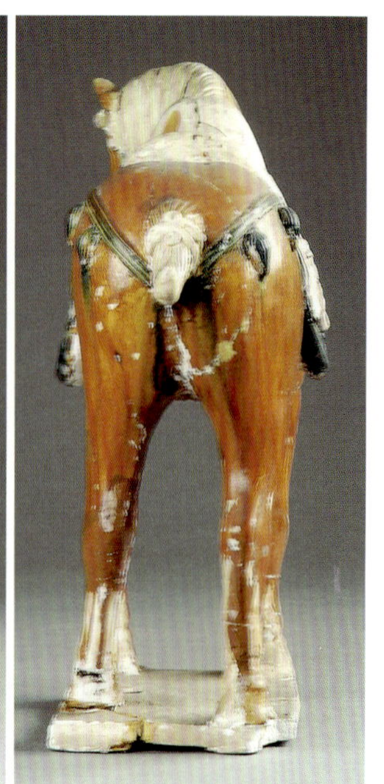

三彩马

陶器

二级文物

长 42.5 厘米　高 36.1 厘米

Tri-colored white horse

Pottery

Second-class cultural relics

42.5 cm in length　36.1 cm in height

三彩马
陶器
一级文物
长 80 厘米　高 70 厘米

Tri-colored horse
Pottery
First-class cultural relics
80 cm in length　70 cm in height

三彩马

唐代
陶器
一级文物
高79厘米
长83厘米

Tri-colored horse
Tang Dynasty
Pottery
First-class cultural relics
79 cm in length
83 cm in height

三彩马
唐代
陶器
二级文物
长 58 厘米　宽 21.5 厘米
高 57 厘米

Tri-colored horse
Tang Dynasty
Pottery
Second-class cultural relics
58 cm in length　21.5 cm in width
57 cm in height

黄釉马

唐代	Yellow-glazed horse
陶器	Tang Dynasty
二级文物	Pottery
	Second-class cultural relics
长 52 厘米　宽 14.6 厘米	52 cm in length　14.6 cm in width
高 52 厘米	52 cm in height

三彩蓝釉白斑马

唐代
陶器
一级文物
纵 36 厘米　横 13 厘米
高 32.5 厘米

Tri-colored blue-glazed horse with white dots
Tang Dynasty
Pottery
First-class cultural relics
36 cm in length　13 cm in width
32.5 cm in height

三彩障泥白釉马

唐代

陶器

一级文物

纵 74 厘米　横 22.8 厘米

高 73.1 厘米

Tri-colored white-glazed horse

Tang Dynasty

Pottery

First-class cultural relics

74 cm in length　22.8 cm in width

73.1 cm in height

三彩马
唐代
陶器
二级文物
长 50 厘米　宽 14.5 厘米
高 49 厘米

Tri-colored horse
Tang Dynasty
Pottery
Second-class cultural relics
50 cm in length　14.5 cm in width
49 cm in height

三彩马

唐代 Tri-colored horse
陶器 Tang Dynasty
Pottery
二级文物 Second-class cultural relics
长 47 厘米 宽 12 厘米 47 cm in length 12 cm in width
高 44 厘米 44 cm in height

三彩马	
唐代	Tri-colored horse
陶器	Tang Dynasty
二级文物	Pottery
	Second-class cultural relics
长 66 厘米　宽 16.5 厘米	66 cm in length　16.5 cm in width
高 63 厘米	63 cm in height

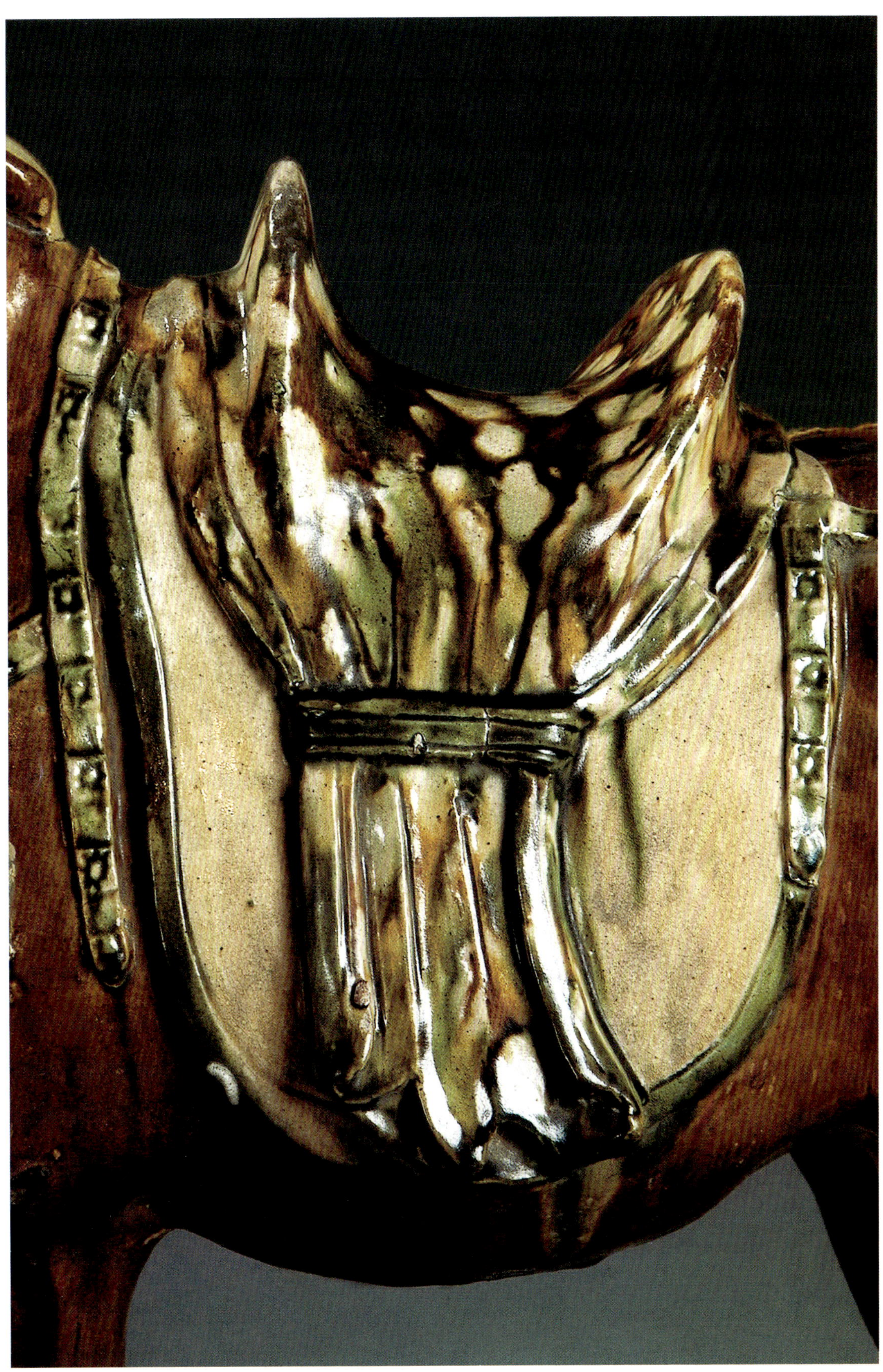

黄釉马
唐代
陶器
二级文物
长 47 厘米　宽 12.6 厘米
高 50 厘米

Yellow- glazed horse
Tang Dynasty
Pottery
Second-class cultural relics
47 cm in length　12.6 cm in width
50 cm in height

白釉马

唐代	White-glazed horse
陶器	Tang Dynasty
二级文物	Pottery
	Second-class cultural relics
长 47 厘米　宽 13 厘米	47 cm in length　13 cm in width
高 51 厘米	51 cm in height

三彩贴宝相花马

三彩贴宝相花马	
唐代	Tri-colored horse with magnolia
陶器	Tang Dynasty
一级文物	Pottery
	First-class cultural relics
纵 61 厘米　横 22.8 厘米	61 cm in length　22.8 cm in width
高 60.5 厘米	60.5 cm in height

三彩马

唐代	Tri-colored horse
陶器	Tang Dynasty
	Pottery
一级文物	First-class cultural relics
纵 35 厘米　横 15 厘米	35 cm in length　15 cm in width
高 32 厘米	32 cm in height

三彩马	
唐代	Tri-colored horse
陶器	Tang Dynasty
	Pottery
二级文物	Second-class cultural relics
长 48 厘米　宽 14.3 厘米	48 cm in length　14.3 cm in width
高 50 厘米	50 cm in height

三彩马
唐代
陶器
二级文物
长 48 厘米 宽 14 厘米
高 49 厘米

Tri-colored horse
Tang Dynasty
Pottery
Second-class cultural relics
48 cm in length 14 cm in width
49 cm in height

黄釉马

唐代 | Yellow- glazed horse
陶器 | Tang Dynasty
Pottery
二级文物 | Second-class cultural relics
长 47 厘米　宽 12.5 厘米 | 47 cm in length　12.5 cm in width
高 46 厘米 | 46 cm in height

三彩马
唐代
陶器
二级文物
长 68 厘米　宽 20.5 厘米
高 68 厘米

Tri-colored horse
Tang Dynasty
Pottery
Second-class cultural relics
68 cm in length　20.5 cm in width
68 cm in height

三彩绿障马

唐代	Tri-colored green-saddled horse
陶器	Tang Dynasty
	Pottery
一级文物	First-class cultural relics
纵 84 厘米　厚 31.5 厘米	84 cm in length　31.5 cm in thickness
高 75 厘米	75 cm in height

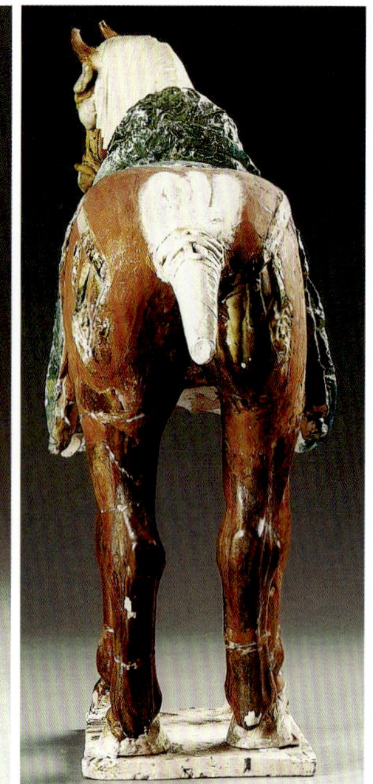

三彩马
唐代
陶器
二级文物
长 50 厘米　高 52 厘米

Tri-colored horse
Tang Dynasty
Pottery
Second-class cultural relics
50 cm in length　52 cm in height

三彩马

陶器

一级文物

长62厘米　高60.5厘米

Tri-colored horse

Pottery

First-class cultural relics

62 cm in length　60.5 cm in height

三彩黑釉马

唐代
陶器
一级文物
纵 84 厘米　横 26 厘米
高 72.5 厘米

Tri-colored black-glazed horse
Tang Dynasty
Pottery
First-class cultural relics
84 cm in length　26 cm in width
72.5 cm in height

三彩马	
唐代	Tri-colored horse
陶器	Tang Dynasty
二级文物	Pottery
	Second-class cultural relics
长 59.5 厘米　宽 21.3 厘米	59.5 cm in length　21.3 cm in width
高 60 厘米	60 cm in height

三彩贴杏叶饰白釉马

唐代	Tri-colored white-glazed horse
陶器	Tang Dynasty
一级文物	Pottery
	First-class cultural relics
纵 82 厘米　横 28 厘米	82 cm in length　28 cm in width
高 75 厘米	75 cm in height

动物俑

骆驼俑

三彩骆驼
唐代
陶器
一级文物
纵 69.7 厘米　横 28.4 厘米
高 81.2 厘米

Tri-colored camel
Tang Dynasty
Pottery
First-class cultural relics
69.7 cm in length　28.4 cm in width
81.2 cm in height

三彩骆驼

唐代
陶器
一级文物
高 87 厘米　长 67 厘米

Tri-colored camel
Tang Dynasty
Pottery
First-class cultural relics
87 cm in height　67 cm in length

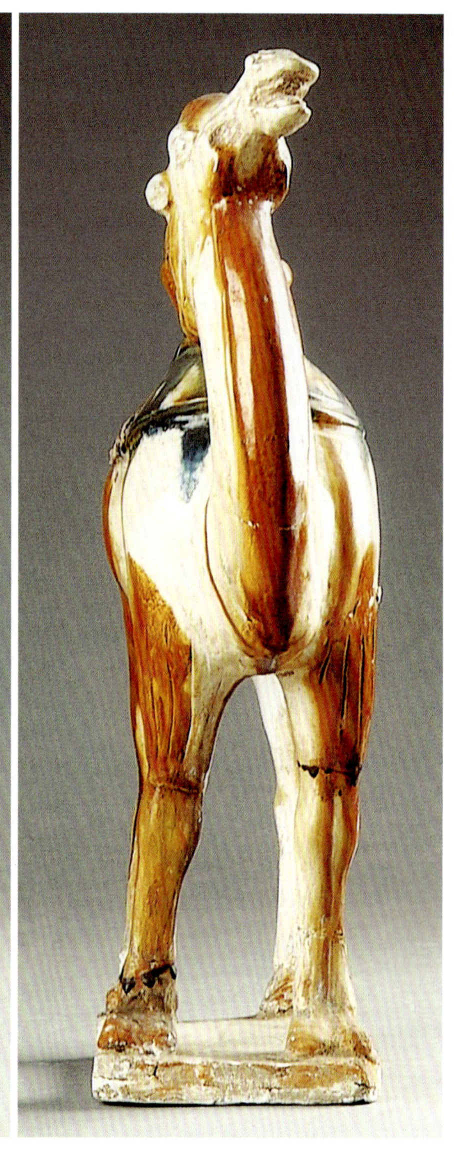

三彩骆驼
唐代
陶器
二级文物
高 40.7 厘米　长 32.5 厘米

Tri-colored camel
Tang Dynasty
Pottery
Second-class cultural relics
40.7 cm in height 32.5 cm in length

三彩骆驼

唐代

陶器

一级文物

长 75 厘米　高 88 厘米

Tri-colored camel

Tang Dynasty

Pottery

First-class cultural relics

75 cm in length　88 cm in height

三彩骆驼
唐代
陶器
一级文物
纵65厘米 横26厘米
高82厘米

Tri-colored camel
Tang Dynasty
Pottery
First-class cultural relics
65 cm in length 26 cm in width
82 cm in height

三彩骆驼

唐代
陶器
二级文物
长 43 厘米　宽 14.5 厘米
高 60 厘米

Tri-colored camel
Tang Dynasty
Pottery
Second-class cultural relics
43 cm in length　14.5 cm in width
60 cm in height

三彩骆驼
唐代
陶器
二级文物
长 42 厘米　高 63 厘米

Tri-colored camel
Tang Dynasty
Pottery
Second-class cultural relics
42 cm in length　63 cm in height

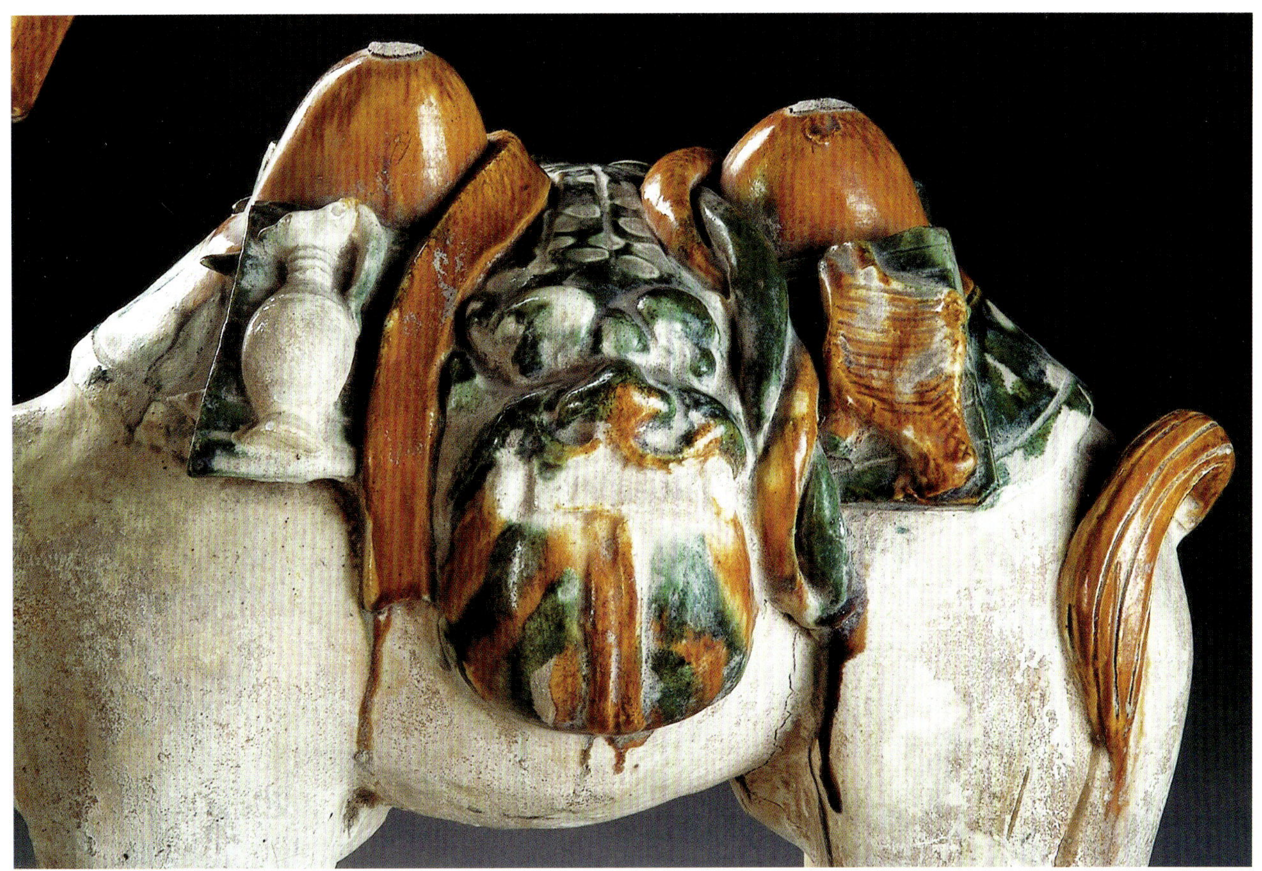

三彩骆驼

唐代	Tri-colored camel
陶器	Tang Dynasty
二级文物	Pottery
	Second-class cultural relics
长 39 厘米　宽 15 厘米	39 cm in length　15 cm in width
高 64 厘米	64 cm in height

三彩骆驼

唐代	Tri-colored camel
陶器	Tang Dynasty
	Pottery
二级文物	Second-class cultural relics
长37厘米　宽14厘米	37 cm in length　14 cm in width
高55厘米	55 cm in height

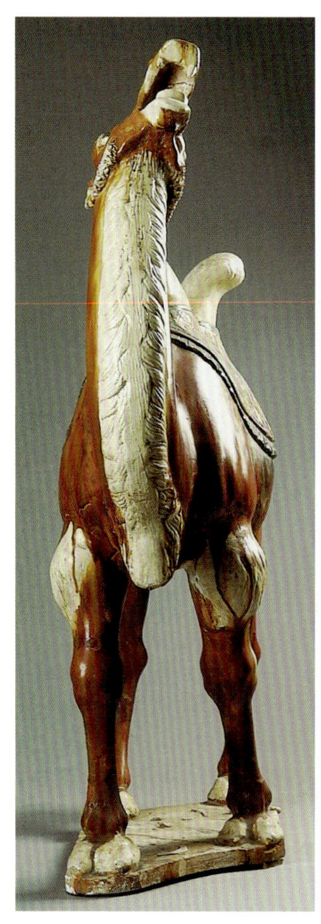

三彩嘶鸣骆驼

唐代
陶器
一级文物
高 88 厘米　长 72.5 厘米
底径 41 厘米

Tri-colored neighing camel
Tang Dynasty
Pottery
First-class cultural relics
88 cm in height　72.5 cm in length
41 cm of bottom diameter

绿釉载丝骆驼

唐代

陶器

一级文物

长 49.5 厘米　高 49.5 厘米

Green — glazed silk-carrying camel

Tang Dynasty

Pottery

First-class cultural relics

49.5 cm in height　49.5 cm in length

三彩骆驼
唐代
陶器
二级文物
长 36 厘米 宽 12 厘米
高 51 厘米

Tri-colored camel
Tang Dynasty
Pottery
Second-class cultural relics
36 cm in length 12 cm in width
51 cm in height

三彩骆驼

唐代
陶器
二级文物
长 31 厘米　宽 9.5 厘米
高 37.5 厘米

Tri-colored camel
Tang Dynasty
Pottery
Second-class cultural relics
31 cm in length　9.5 cm in width
37.5 cm in height

三彩骆驼

唐代
陶器
二级文物
长 39 厘米　宽 13.6 厘米
高 51 厘米

Tri-colored camel
Tang Dynasty
Pottery
Second-class cultural relics
39 cm in length　13.6 cm in width
51 cm in height

三彩骆驼

唐代

陶器

二级文物

长 42 厘米　宽 15 厘米

高 63 厘米

Tri-colored camel

Tang Dynasty

Pottery

Second-class cultural relics

42 cm in length　15 cm in width

63 cm in height

三彩骆驼

唐代
陶器
二级文物
长 42 厘米　宽 15.3 厘米
高 64 厘米

Tri-colored camel
Tang Dynasty
Pottery
Second-class cultural relics
42 cm in length　15.3 cm in width
64 cm in height

三彩载丝骆驼

唐代	Tri-colored silk -carrying camel
陶器	Tang Dynasty
二级文物	Pottery
	Second-class cultural relics
高66厘米	66 cm in height

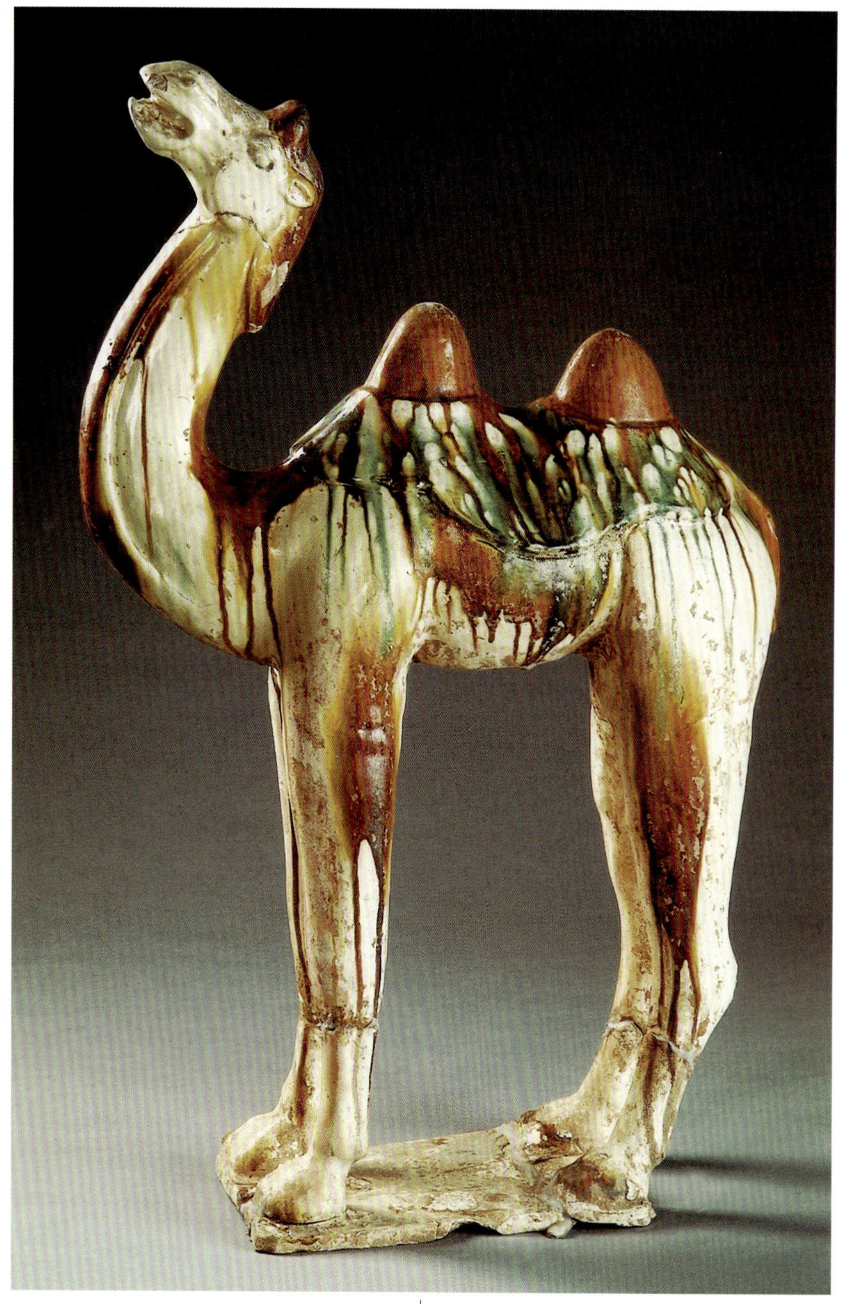

三彩骆驼	
唐代	Tri-colored camel
陶器	Tang Dynasty
二级文物	Pottery
长40厘米　宽15厘米	Second-class cultural relics
高55厘米	40 cm in length　15 cm in width
	55 cm in height

B88 三彩骆驼

唐代	Tri-colored camel
陶器	Tang Dynasty
	Pottery
二级文物	Second-class cultural relics
长 46 厘米 宽 16.4 厘米	46 cm in length 16.4 cm in width
高 61 厘米	61 cm in height

三彩骆驼
唐代
陶器
二级文物
长 46 厘米　宽 16.5 厘米
高 66 厘米

Tri-colored camel
Tang Dynasty
Pottery
Second-class cultural relics
46 cm in length　16.5 cm in width
66 cm in height

三彩骆驼

唐代	Tri-colored camel
陶器	Tang Dynasty
	Pottery
二级文物	Second-class cultural relics
长 40 厘米　宽 14.1 厘米	40 cm in length　14.1 cm in width
高 57 厘米	57 cm in height

三彩长腿骆驼

唐代
陶器
二级文物
长41厘米　高62厘米

Tri-colored camel with long legs
Tang Dynasty
Pottery
Second-class cultural relics
41 cm in length　62 cm in height

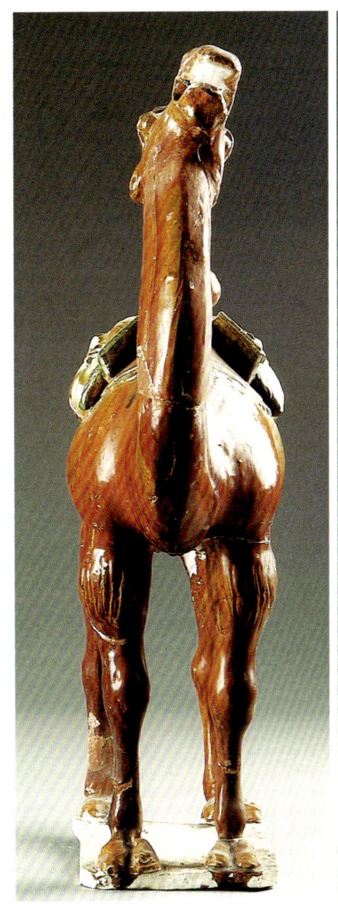

三彩骆驼
唐代
陶器
二级文物
高60厘米

Tri-colored camel
Tang Dynasty
Pottery
Second-class cultural relics
60 cm in height

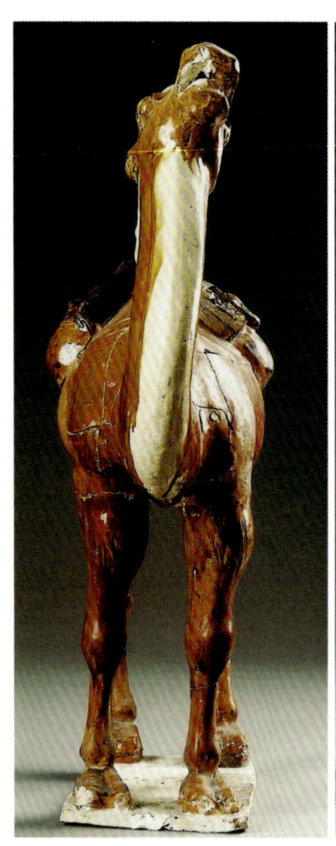

三彩骆驼

唐代
陶器
二级文物
高58厘米

Tri-colored camel
Tang Dynasty
Pottery
Second-class cultural relics
58 cm in height

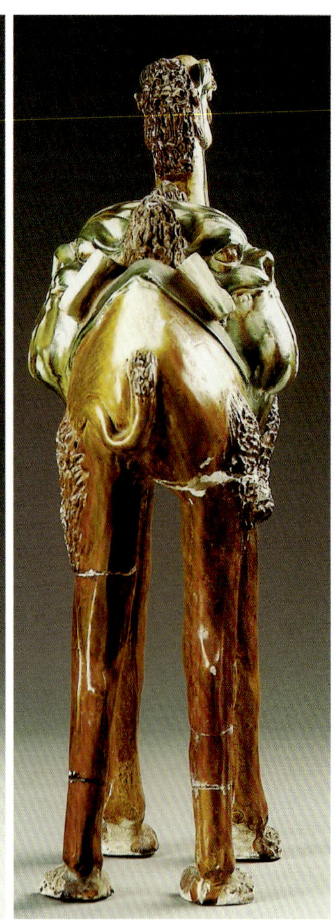

三彩骆驼

唐代	Tri-colored camel
陶器	Tang Dynasty
二级文物	Pottery
高51厘米	Second-class cultural relics
	51 cm in height

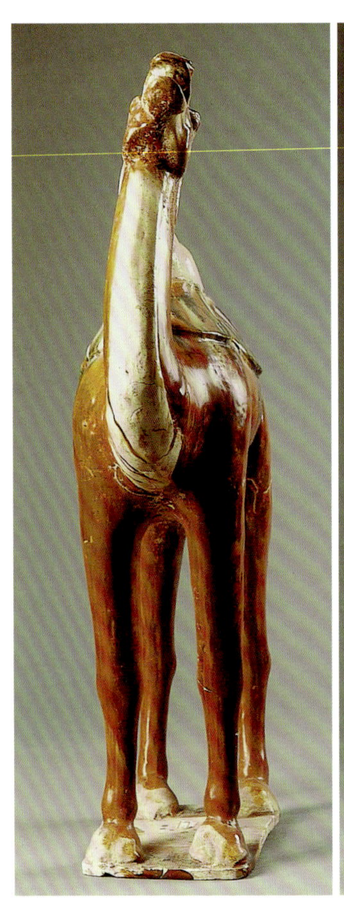

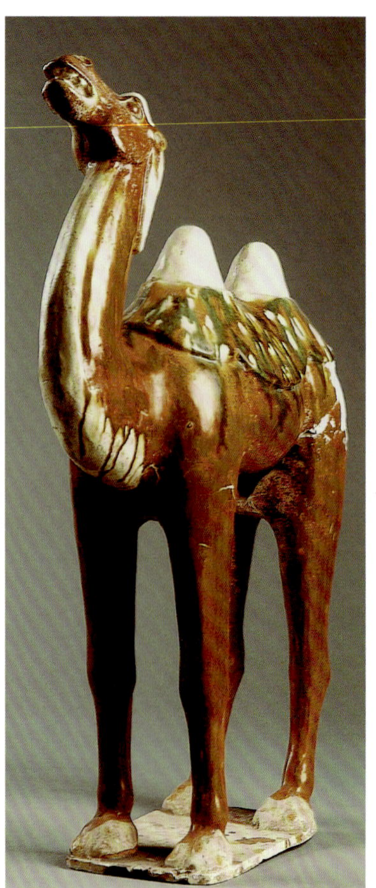

三彩骆驼
唐代
陶器
二级文物
高 66 厘米　长 41 厘米

Tri-colored camel
Tang Dynasty
Pottery
Second-class cultural relics
66 cm in height　41 cm in length

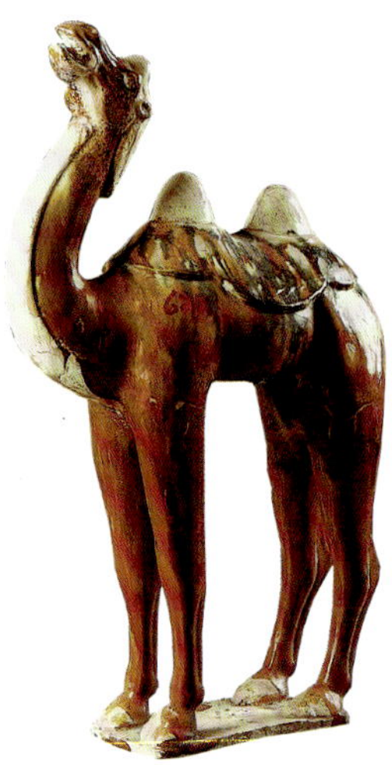

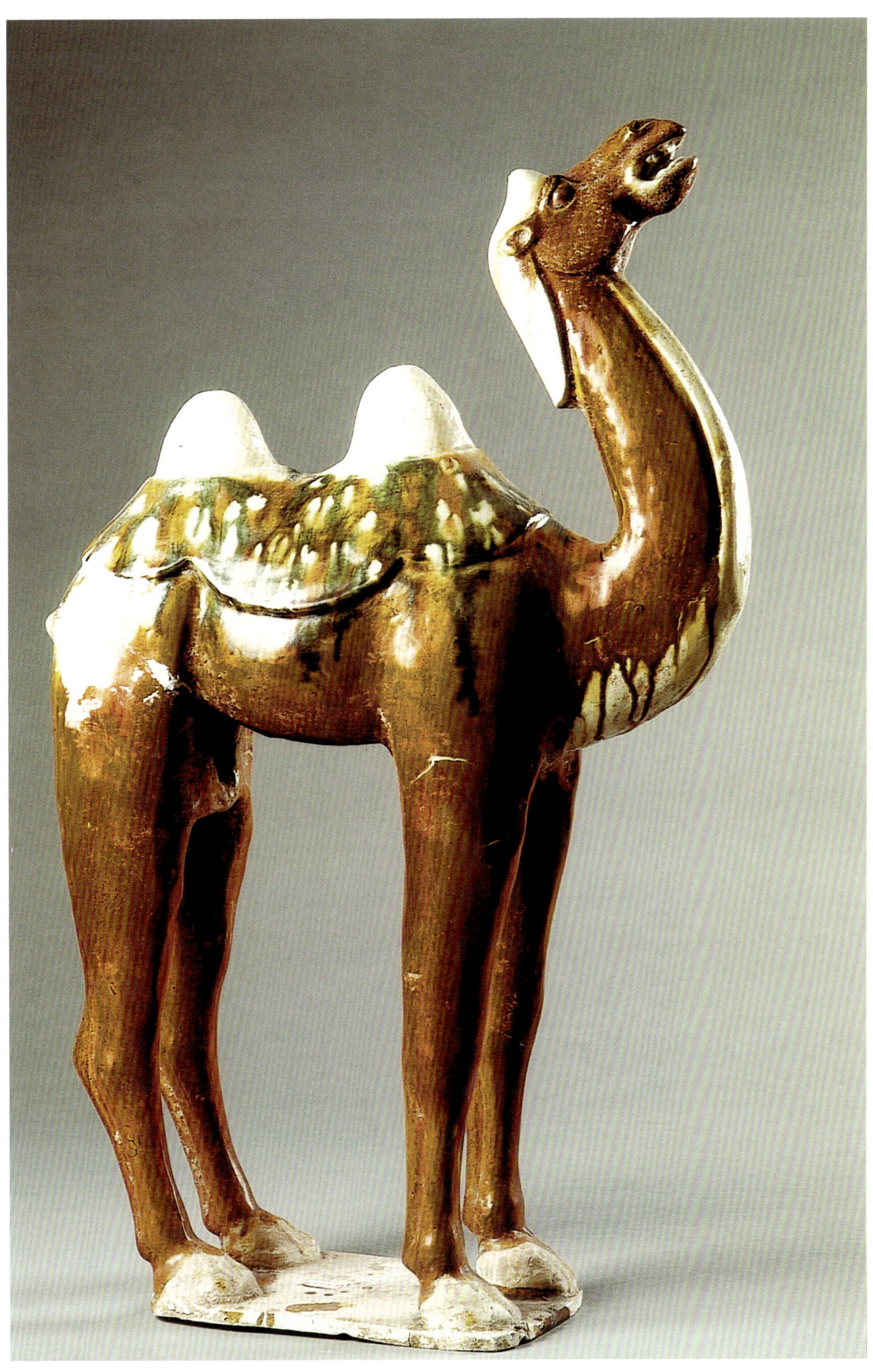

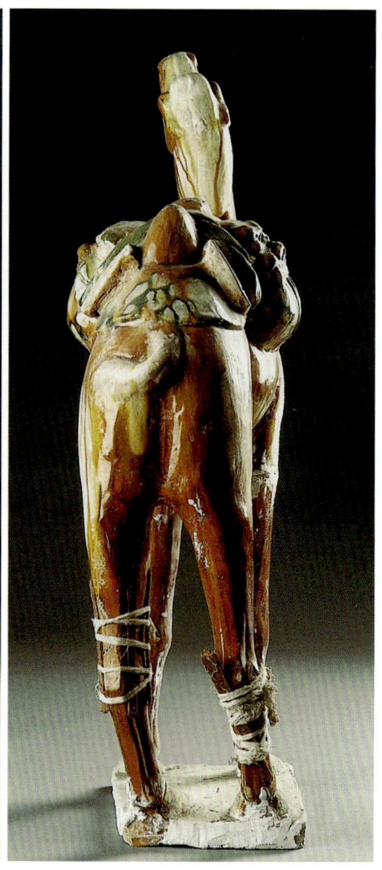

三彩骆驼
唐代
陶器
二级文物
纵 40 厘米　横 20 厘米
高 66 厘米

Tri-colored camel
Tang Dynasty
Pottery
Second-class cultural relics
40 cm in length　20 cm in width
66 cm in height

三彩兽头驼包骆驼

唐代

陶器

一级文物

纵 68 厘米　横 25 厘米

高 84 厘米

Tri-colored beast-head camel

Tang Dynasty

Pottery

Second-class cultural relics

68 cm in length　25 cm in width

84 cm in height

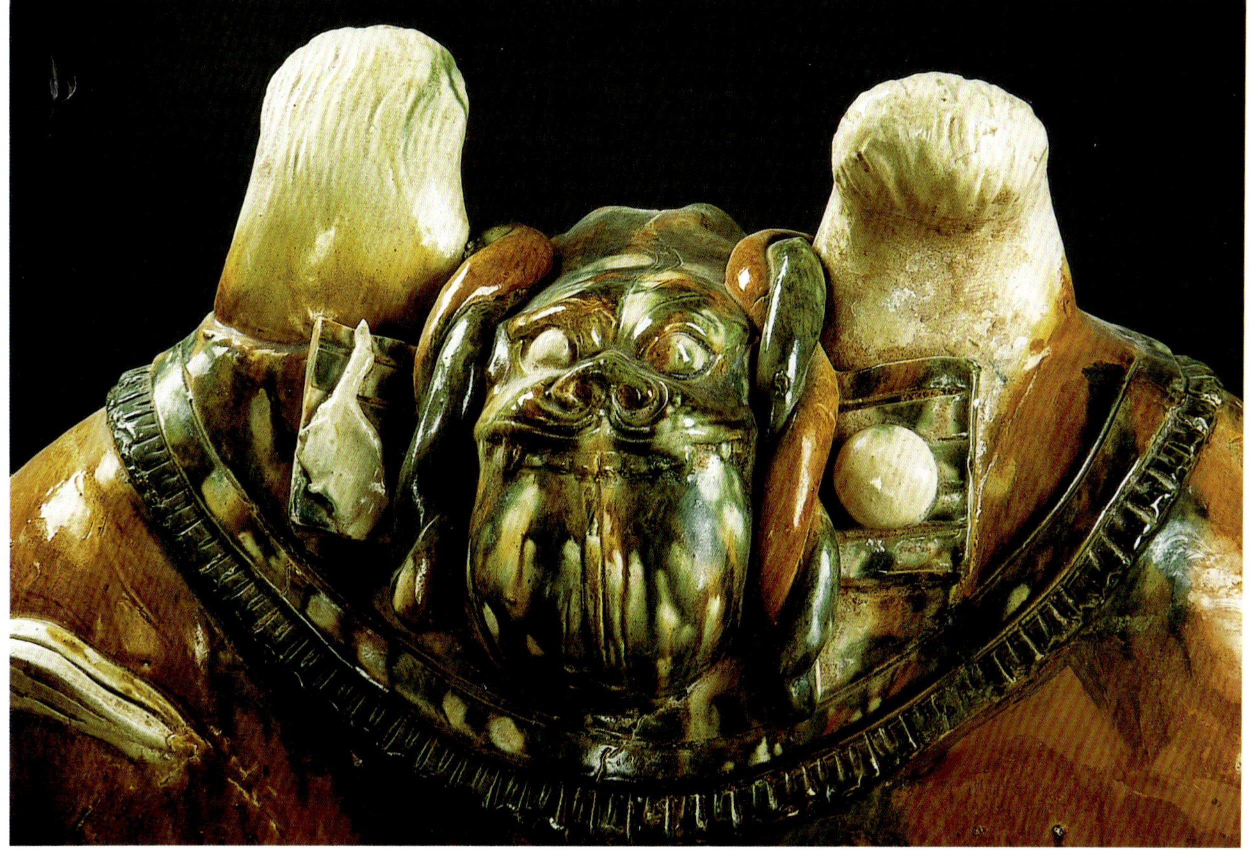

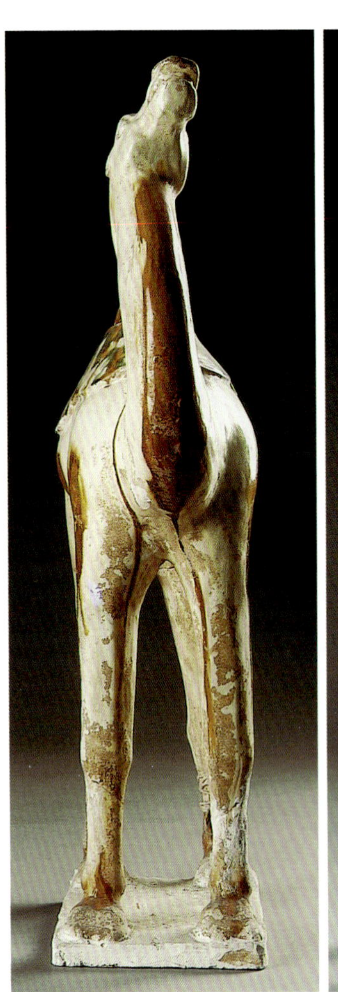

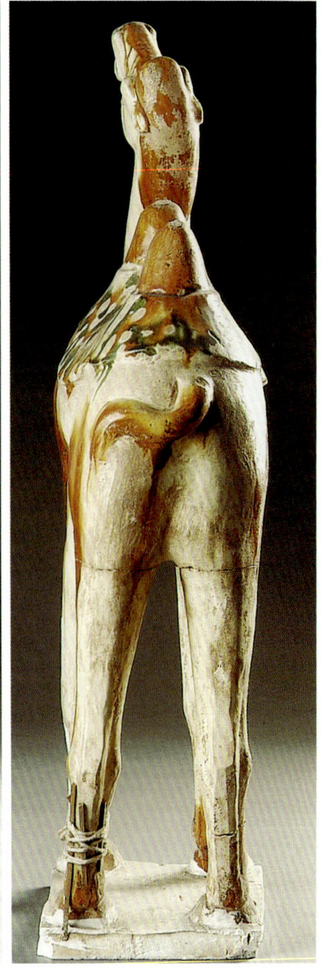

三彩骆驼
唐代
陶器
二级文物
纵 43 厘米 横 16 厘米
高 66.5 厘米

Tri-colored camel
Tang Dynasty
Pottery
Second-class cultural relics
43 cm in length 16 cm in width
66.5 cm in height

动物俑

镇墓兽

三彩镇墓兽

唐代 | Tri-colored animality patron in tomb

陶器 | Tang Dynasty

一级文物 | Pottery

First-class cultural relics

宽16厘米　最厚14厘米 | 16 cm in width　14 cm in thickness

高56.5厘米 | 56.5 cm in height

三彩兽面镇墓兽
唐代
陶器
一级文物
高 96 厘米　宽 39 厘米

Tri-colored beast- face animality patron in tomb
Tang Dynasty
Pottery
First-class cultural relics
96 cm in height　39 cm in width

三彩人面镇墓兽

唐代 Tri-colored human-face animality patron in tomb

陶器 Tang Dynasty

一级文物 Pottery

First-class cultural relics

高104厘米 宽35厘米 104 cm in height 35 cm in width

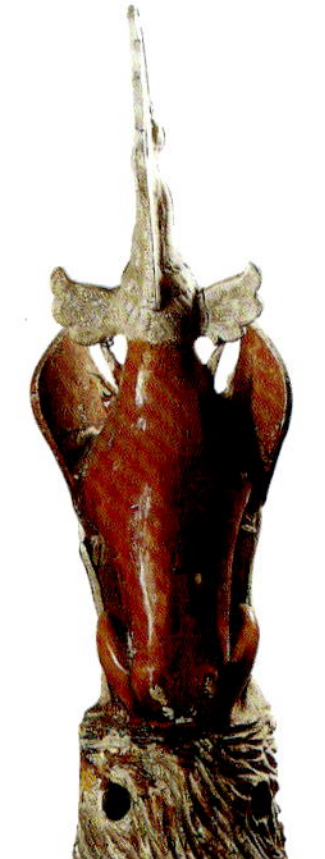

三彩镇墓兽

唐代	Tri-colored animality patron in tomb
陶器	Tang Dynasty
一级文物	Pottery
高103.5厘米	First-class cultural relics
	103.5 cm in height

三彩镇墓兽

唐代	Tri-colored animality patron in tomb
陶器	Tang Dynasty
二级文物	Pottery
通高87厘米	Second-class cultural relics
	87 cm in height

三彩镇墓兽

唐代

陶器

二级文物

长 23 厘米　宽 17 厘米

高 64 厘米

Tri-colored animality patron in tomb

Tang Dynasty

Pottery

Second-class cultural relics

23 cm in length　17 cm in width

64 cm in height

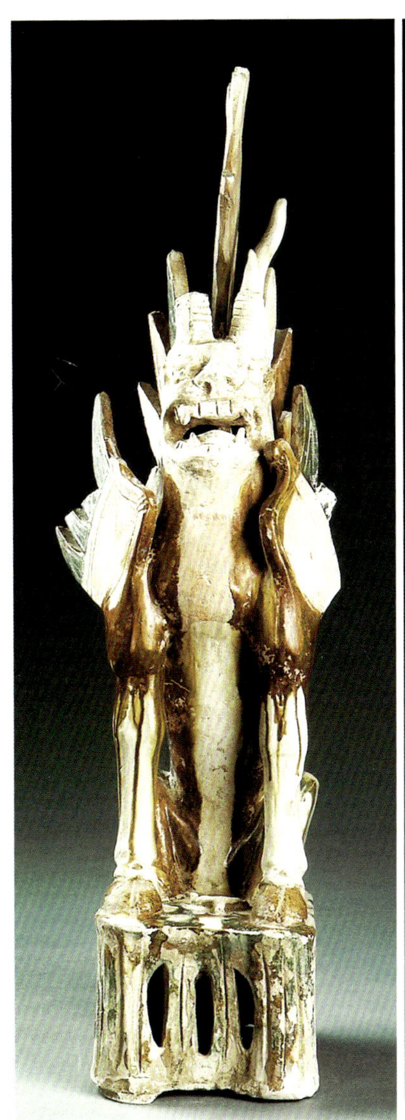

三彩镇墓兽

唐代 | Tri-colored animality patron in tomb
陶器 | Tang Dynasty
二级文物 | Pottery
Second-class cultural relics
长23厘米　宽19.5厘米 | 23 cm in length　19.5 cm in width
高70厘米 | 70 cm in height

三彩镇墓兽

唐代 Tri-colored animality patron in tomb

陶器 Tang Dynasty

二级文物 Pottery

Second-class cultural relics

长 22.5 厘米 宽 16.5 厘米 22.5 cm in length 16.5 cm in width

高 72 厘米 72 cm in height

三彩兽面镇墓兽
唐代
陶器
一级文物
通高103厘米

Tri-colored beast-face animality patron in tomb
Tang Dynasty
Pottery
First-class cultural relics
103 cm in height

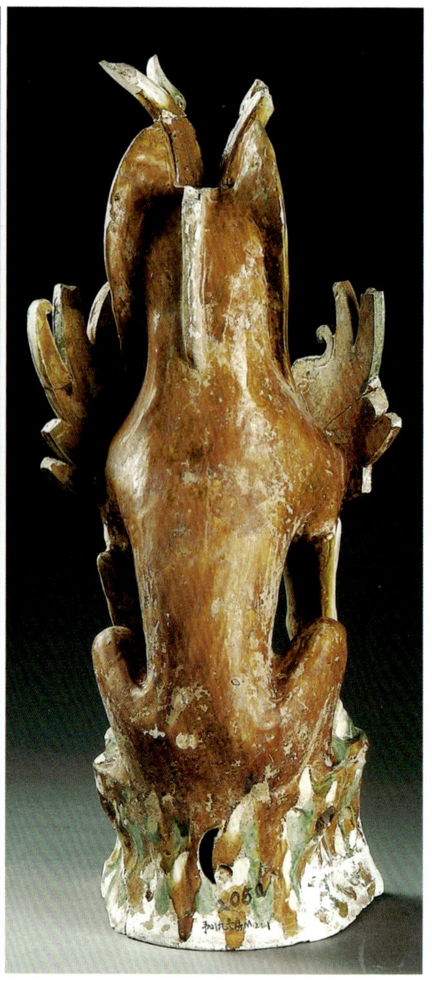

三彩镇墓兽

唐代
陶器
二级文物
长29厘米　宽25厘米
高68厘米

Tri-colored animality patron in tomb
Tang Dynasty
Pottery
Second-class cultural relics
29 cm in length　25 cm in width
68 cm in height

三彩镇墓兽

唐代	Tri-colored animality patron in tomb
陶器	Tang Dynasty
二级文物	Pottery
	Second-class cultural relics
长 21 厘米　宽 20 厘米	21 cm in length　20 cm in width
高 71 厘米	71 cm in height

三彩镇墓兽	
唐代	Tri-colored animality patron in tomb
陶器	Tang Dynasty
二级文物	Pottery
	Second-class cultural relics
长 12.5 厘米　宽 10 厘米	12.5 cm in length　10 cm in width
高 39.5 厘米	39.5 cm in height

三彩镇墓兽

唐代
陶器
二级文物
长 24 厘米　宽 20 厘米
高 75 厘米

Tri-colored animality patron in tomb
Tang Dynasty
Pottery
Second-class cultural relics
24 cm in length　20 cm in width
75 cm in height

三彩镇墓兽

唐代	Tri-colored animality patron in tomb
陶器	Tang Dynasty
二级文物	Pottery
	Second-class cultural relics
长23厘米　宽18厘米	23 cm in length　18 cm in width
高71厘米	71 cm in height

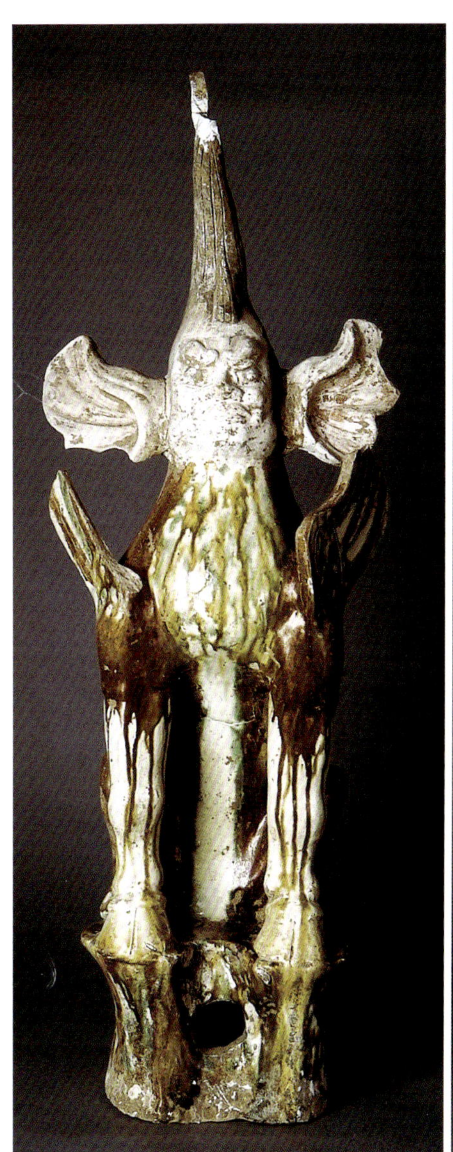

三彩镇墓兽

唐代

陶器

二级文物

长 25 厘米　宽 16 厘米

高 72 厘米

Tri-colored animality patron in tomb

Tang Dynasty

Pottery

Second-class cultural relics

25 cm in length　16 cm in width

72 cm in height

三彩人面镇墓兽

唐代 | Tri-colored human-face animality patron in tomb

陶器 | Tang Dynasty

一级文物 | Pottery

通高 103.5 厘米 | First-class cultural relics

103.5 cm in general height

三彩镇墓兽

唐代	Tri-colored animality patron in tomb
陶器	Tang Dynasty
二级文物	Pottery
高108厘米	Second-class cultural relics
	108 cm in height

三彩镇墓兽

唐代
陶器
二级文物
长 22.5 厘米　宽 17.5 厘米
高 63 厘米

Tri-colored animality patron in tomb
Tang Dynasty
Pottery
Second-class cultural relics
22.5 cm in length　17.5 cm in width
63 cm in height

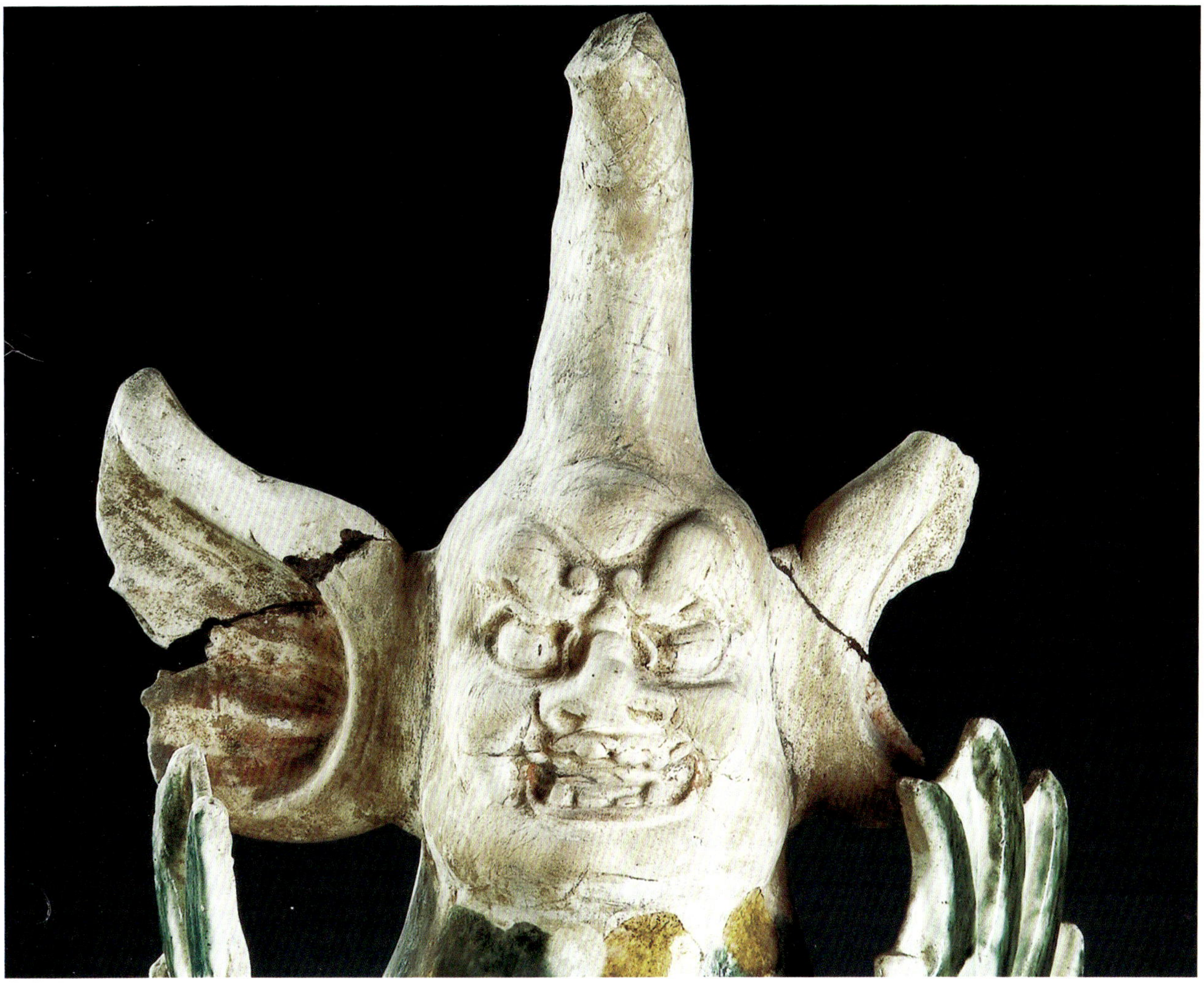

三彩镇墓兽

唐代
陶器
二级文物
长 22.5 厘米　宽 16.5 厘米
高 64 厘米

Tri-colored animality patron in tomb
Tang Dynasty
Pottery
Second-class cultural relics
22.5 cm in length　16.5 cm in width
64 cm in height

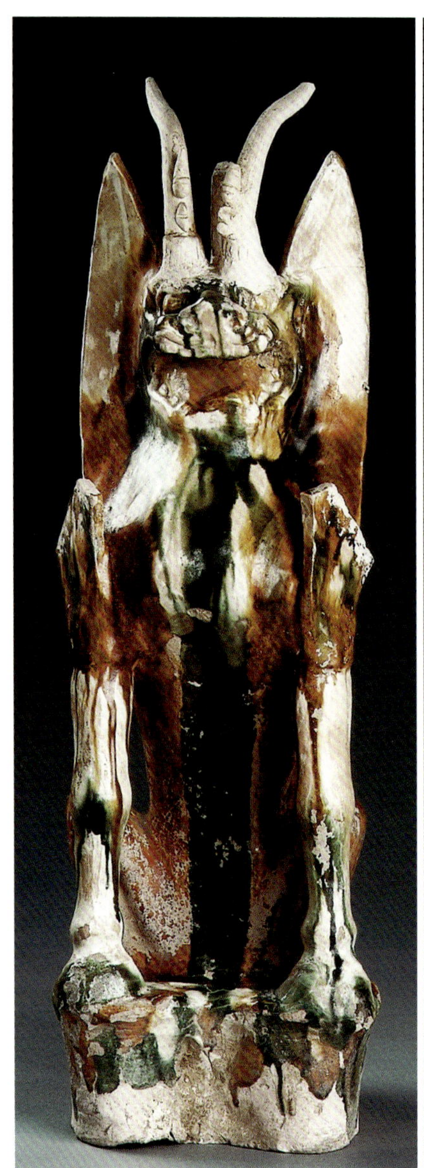

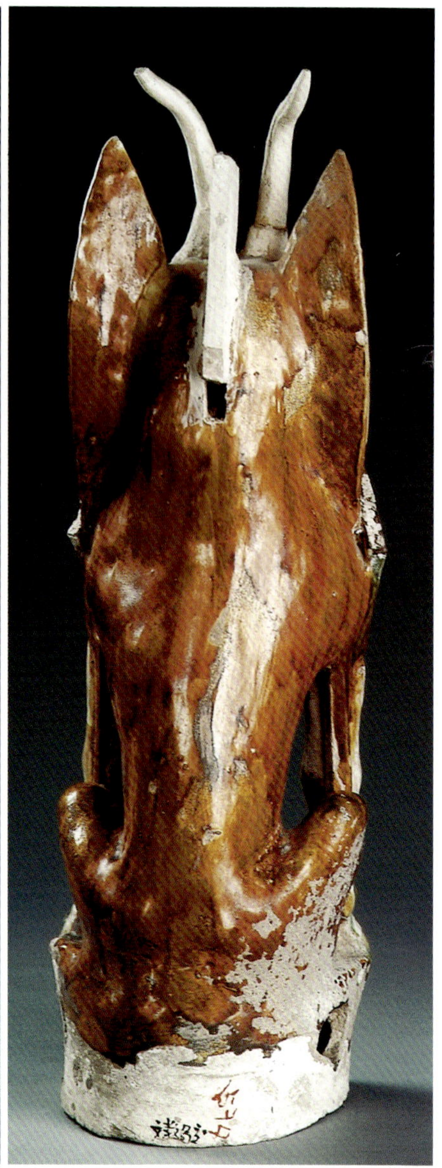

三彩镇墓兽	
唐代	Tri-colored animality patron in tomb
陶器	Tang Dynasty
二级文物	Pottery
	Second-class cultural relics
长 23.5 厘米　宽 16 厘米	23.5 cm in length　16 cm in width
高 62 厘米	62 cm in height

三彩镇墓兽
唐代
陶器
二级文物
长 23 厘米　宽 10.5 厘米
高 65.5 厘米

Tri-colored animality patron in tomb
Tang Dynasty
Pottery
Second-class cultural relics
23 cm in length　10.5 cm in width
65.5 cm in height

三彩镇墓兽	
唐代	Tri-colored animality patron in tomb
陶器	Tang Dynasty
二级文物	Pottery
长 24 厘米　宽 36 厘米	Second-class cultural relics
高 93 厘米	24 cm in length　36 cm in width
	93 cm in height

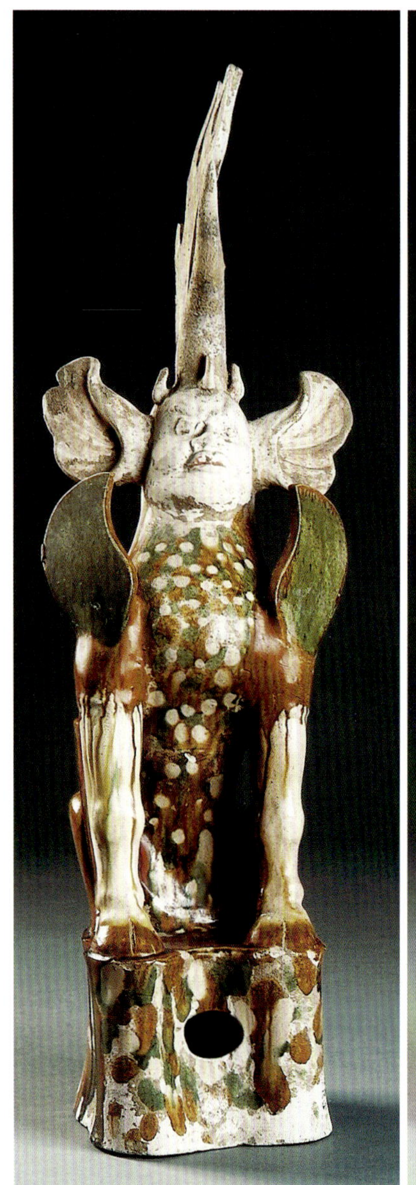

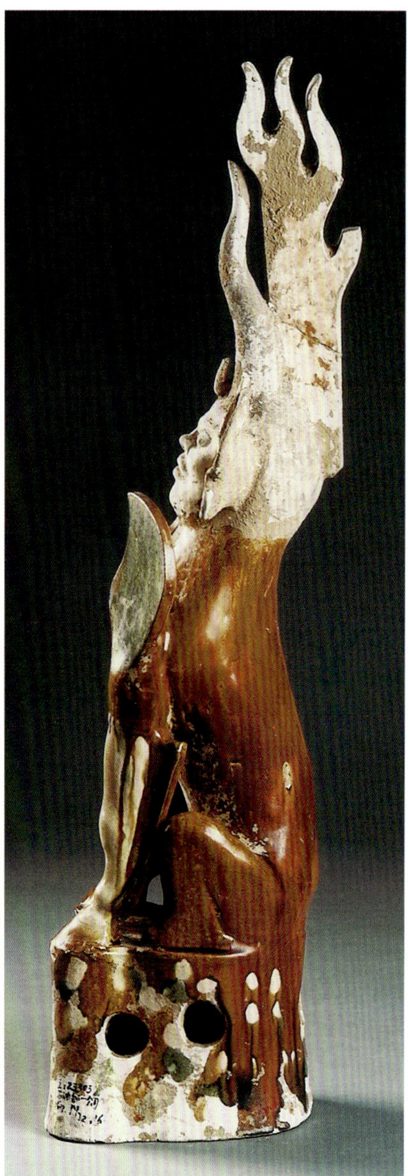

三彩镇墓兽

唐代　Tri-colored animality patron in tomb
陶器　Tang Dynasty
二级文物　Pottery
高 74 厘米　Second-class cultural relics
74 cm in height

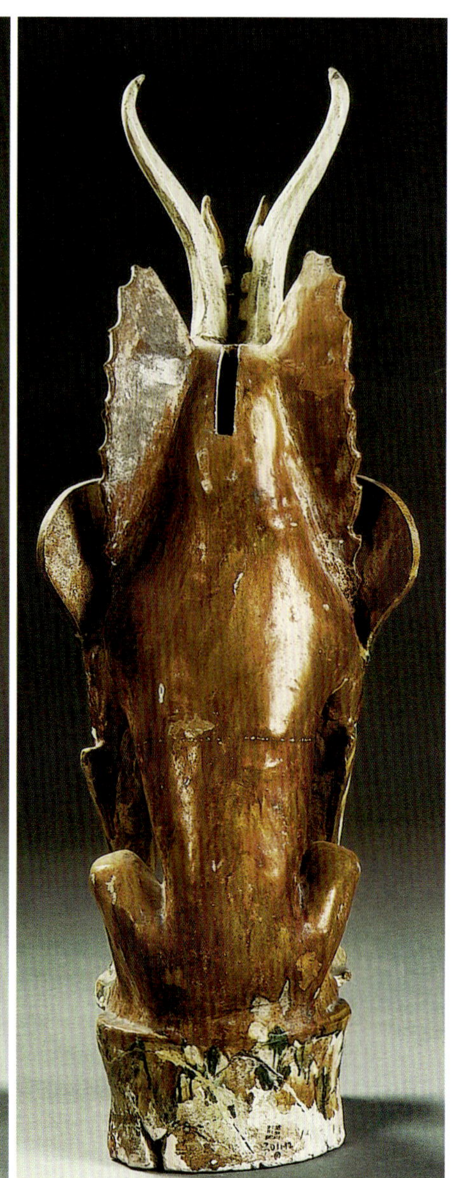

三彩兽面镇墓兽

唐代
陶器
一级文物
宽33.5厘米　厚26.3厘米
高90.5厘米

Tri-colored beast-face animality patron in tomb
Tang Dynasty
Pottery
First-class cultural relics
33.5 cm in width　26.3 cm in thickness
90.5 cm in height

三彩镇墓兽

唐代　Tri-colored animality patron in tomb
陶器　Tang Dynasty
二级文物　Pottery
Second-class cultural relics
长 22 厘米　宽 18 厘米　22 cm in length　18 cm in width
高 79 厘米　79 cm in height

三彩镇墓兽

唐代 Tri-colored animality patron in tomb
陶器 Tang Dynasty
二级文物 Pottery
Second-class cultural relics
高 74 厘米 74 cm in height

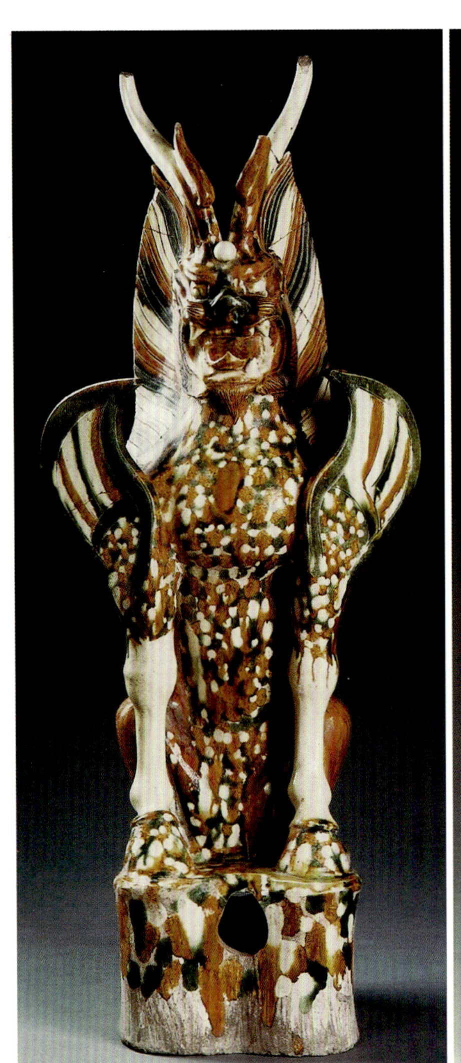

三彩镇墓兽	
唐代	Tri-colored animality patron in tomb
陶器	Tang Dynasty
二级文物	Pottery
	Second-class cultural relics
长 35 厘米　宽 23.5 厘米	35 cm in length　23.5 cm in width
高 84 厘米	84 cm in height

三彩镇墓兽

唐代
陶器
二级文物
长 23.5 厘米 宽 20 厘米
高 57 厘米

Tri-colored animality patron in tomb
Tang Dynasty
Pottery
Second-class cultural relics
23.5 cm in length 20 cm in width
57 cm in height

三彩镇墓兽
唐代
陶器
二级文物
高 63 厘米

Tri-colored animality patron in tomb
Tang Dynasty
Pottery
Second-class cultural relics
63 cm in height

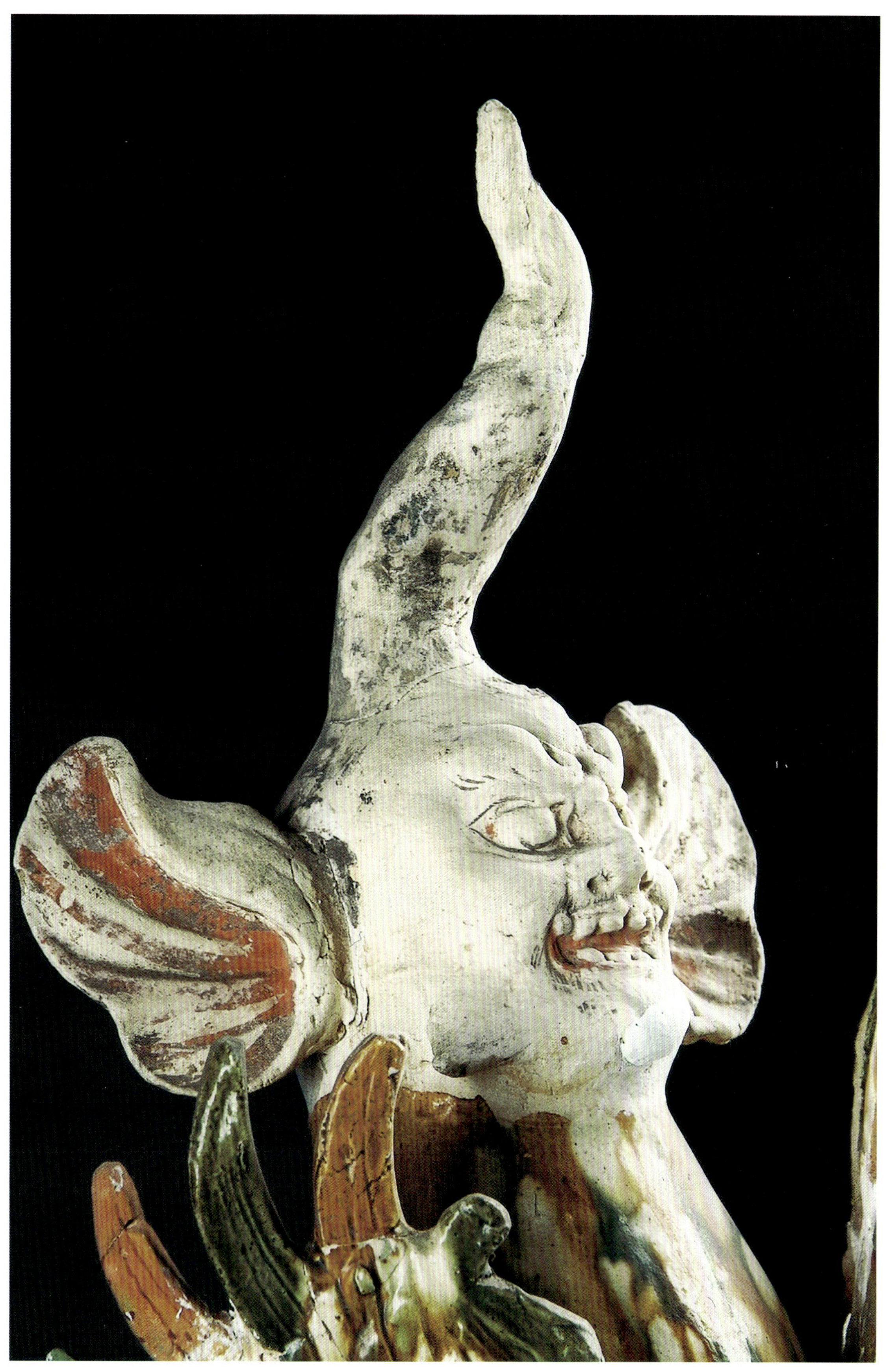

三彩镇墓兽	
陶器	Tri-colored animality patron in tomb
二级文物	Pottery
	Second-class cultural relics
上部最宽 19 厘米	19 cm of the upper width
高 65 厘米	65 cm in height
腹围 50 厘米	50 cm of bully diameter

三彩人面镇墓兽

唐代

陶器

二级文物

宽 39 厘米　厚 27 厘米

高 88 厘米

Tri-colored human-face animality patron in tomb

Tang Dynasty

Pottery

Second-class cultural relics

39 cm in width　27 cm in thickness

88 cm in height

三彩镇墓兽

唐代 Tri-colored animality patron in tomb

陶器 Tang Dynasty

二级文物 Pottery

高 69 厘米 Second-class cultural relics

69 cm in height

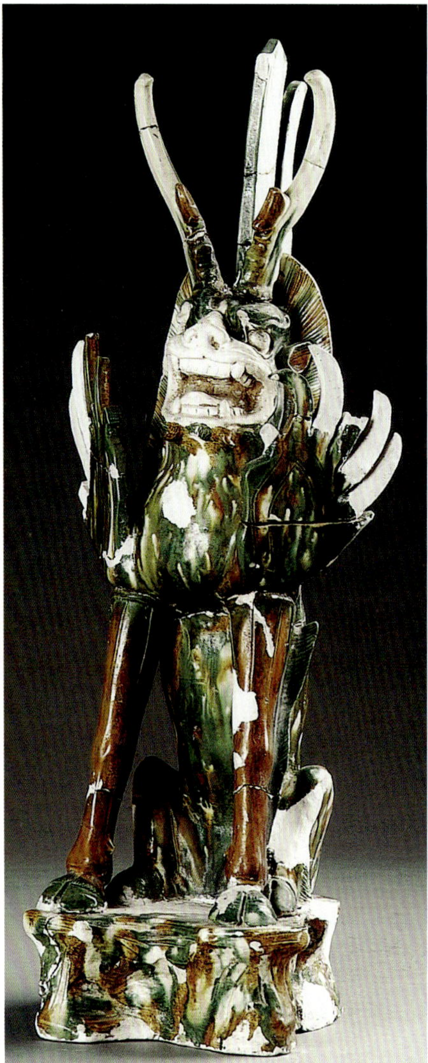

三彩镇墓兽

唐代	Tri-colored animality patron in tomb
陶器	Tang Dynasty
二级文物	Pottery
高 69.5 厘米	Second-class cultural relics
	69.5 cm in height

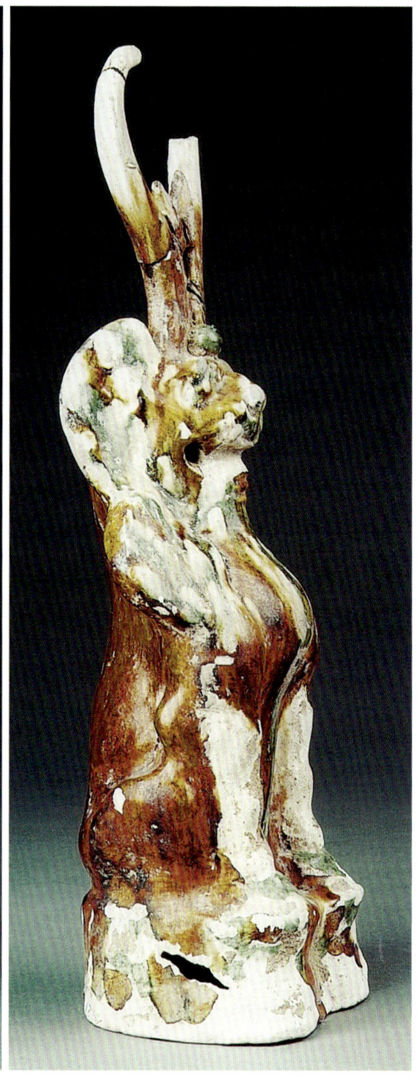

三彩镇墓兽

陶器

二级文物

高35厘米

宽12.8厘米

Tri-colored animality patron in tomb

Pottery

Second-class cultural relics

35 cm in height

12.8cm in width

三彩镇墓兽

陶器
二级文物
高36厘米

Tri-colored animality patron in tomb
Pottery
Second-class cultural relics
36 cm in height

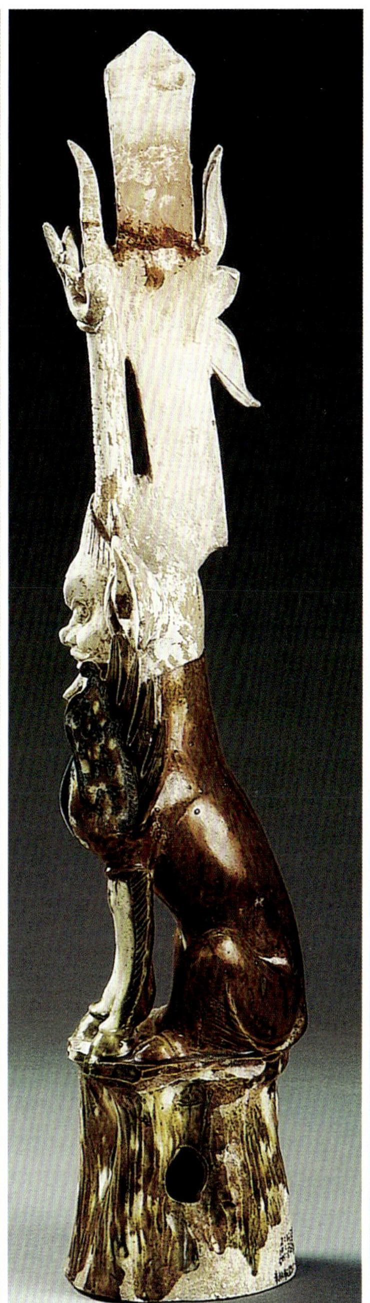

三彩人面镇墓兽

唐代	Tri-colored human-face animality patron in tomb
陶器	Tang Dynasty
一级文物	Pottery
纵 13.7 厘米　厚 14 厘米	First-class cultural relics
高 59.4 厘米	13.7 cm in length　14 cm in thickness
	59.4 cm in height

三彩镇墓兽

陶器	Tri-colored animality patron in tomb
二级文物	Pottery
上部最宽14厘米	Second-class cultural relics
高38厘米	14 cm of the upper width
	38 cm in height

三彩镇墓兽

唐代	Tri-colored animality patron in tomb
陶器	Tang Dynasty
二级文物	Pottery
通高65.5厘米	Second-class cultural relics
	65.5 cm in height

三彩镇墓兽
唐代
陶器
二级文物
通高80厘米　底座宽21厘米

Tri-colored animality patron in tomb
Tang Dynasty
Pottery
Second-class cultural relics
80 cm in height　21 cm of base width

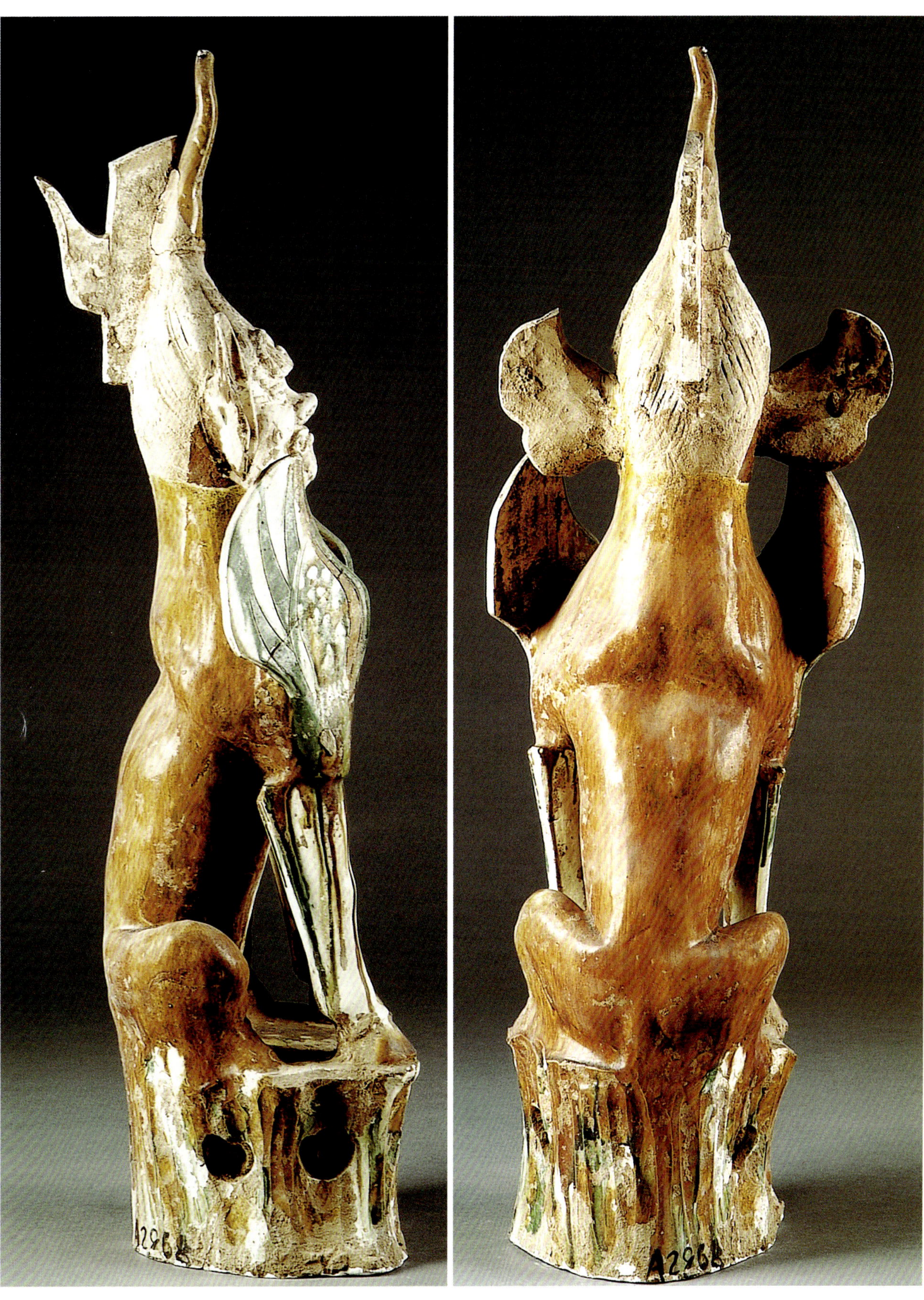

动物俑

其他

三彩黄釉牛
陶器
二级文物
高 13.5 厘米　长 17.4 厘米

Tri-colored yellow-glazed cow
Pottery
Second-class cultural relis
13.5 cm in height　17.4 cm in length

三彩狮子狗	
唐代	Tri-colored pug-dog
陶器	Tang Dynasty
二级文物	Pottery
	Second-class cultural relics
高 7 厘米	7 cm in height
长 5.5 厘米　宽 3.6 厘米	5.5 cm in length　3.6 cm in width

黄釉尖嘴狗

唐代
陶器
一级文物
长 14.2 厘米　高 16 厘米

Yellow-glazed dog with sharp mouth
Tang Dynasty
Pottery
First-class cultural relics
14.2 cm in length　16 cm in height

三彩鸡
陶器
二级文物
高 15 厘米　长 16.5 厘米

Tri-colored cock
Pottery
Second-class cultural relics
15 cm in height　16.5 cm in length

三彩鸡

唐代
陶器
二级文物
长15.5厘米　宽6.5厘米
高16厘米

Tri-colored cock
Tang Dynasty
Pottery
Second-class cultural relics
15.5 cm in length 6.5 cm in width
16 cm in height

三彩白釉黄斑羊
唐代
陶器
二级文物
长 20 厘米　宽 6 厘米
高 13 厘米

Tri-colored white-glazed sheep with yellow spots
Tang Dynasty
Pottery
Second-class cultural relics
20 cm in length　6 cm in width
13 cm in height

生活器物

饮用器

三彩珍珠条纹罐

唐代

陶器

二级文物

高 26.5 厘米　口径 11.8 厘米

底径 11.4 厘米　腹径 23.2 厘米

Tri-colored pearl jar with stripes

Tang Dynasty

Pottery

Second-class cultural relics

26.5 cm in height　11.8cm of caliber

11.4 cm of base diameter

23.2 cm of belly measurement

三彩珍珠纹贴花带盖镀

唐代	Tri-colored pearl-spotted pot with lid
陶器	Tang Dynasty
一级文物	Pottery
高 20 厘米　腹围 70 厘米	First-class cultural relics
口径 12.5 厘米　足距 8 厘米	20 cm in height　70 cm of belly measurement
	12.5 cm of caliber　8 cm between feet

三彩贴宝相花带盖镀

唐代	Tri-colored magnolia-mounted vessel with lid
陶器	Tang Dynasty
二级文物	Pottery
高21厘米	Second-class cultural relics
口径14.5厘米　腹围24厘米	21 cm in height
	14.5 cm of caliber　24 cm of belly measurement

三彩贴花镀

唐代	Tri-colored vessel inlaid with flowers
陶器	Tang Dynasty
一级文物	Pottery
高 20.5 厘米	First-class cultural relics
	20.5 cm in height
腹高 21 厘米　口径 13 厘米	21 cm in height of belly　13 cm of caliber

三彩罐

五代

陶器

二级文物

高16厘米

口径6.8厘米　底径7.6厘米

Tri-colored jar

Five Dynasties

Pottery

Second-class cultural relics

16 cm in height

6.8 cm of caliber　7.6 cm of base diameter

三彩贴花带盖罐

唐代	Tri-colored flowers-mounted jar with lid
陶器	Tang Dynasty
一级文物	Pottery
高30厘米　腹围69厘米	First-class cultural relics
口径10厘米　底径9厘米	30 cm in height　69 cm of belly measurement
	10 cm of caliber　9 cm of base diameter

三彩绿釉条纹罐
唐代
陶器
二级文物
高 24.5 厘米
口径 12.5 厘米

Tri-colored green-glazed jar with stripes
Tang Dynasty
Pottery
Second-class cultural relics
24.5 cm in height
12.5 cm of caliber

杭六香山M1
②

三彩珍珠条纹罐

唐代

陶器

二级文物

高 26.3 厘米　口径 12 厘米

底径 9 厘米

Tri-colored jar with stripes and spots

Tang Dynasty

Pottery

Second-class cultural relics

26.3 cm in height　12 cm of caliber

9 cm of base diameter

三彩珍珠条纹罐

陶器

二级文物

高34厘米

口径11.5厘米

Tri-colored jar with stripes and spots

Pottery

Second-class cultural relics

34 cm in height

11.5 cm of caliber

绿釉罐

五代
陶器
二级文物
高6.5厘米
口径3.5厘米　底径3.5厘米

green-glazed jar
Five Dynasties
Pottery
Second-class cultural relics
6.5 cm in height
3.5 cm of caliber　3.5 cm of base diameter

三彩菱形纹罐
唐代
陶器
一级文物
高29.5厘米　口径12.6厘米
底径12.2厘米　盖径13厘米

Tri-colored jar with thrombus stripes
Tang Dynasty
Pottery
First-class cultural relics
29.5 cm in height　12.6 cm of caliber
12.2 cm of base diameter　13 cm of lid diameter

三彩罐
唐代
陶器
二级文物
口径8.3厘米　高29.6厘米

Tri-colored jar
Tang Dynasty
Pottery
Second-class cultural relics
8.3 cm of caliber　29.6 cm in height

三彩三足罐
唐代
陶器
二级文物
口径 11 厘米　高 12 厘米

Tri-colored jar with three legs
Tang Dynasty
Pottery
Second-class cultural relics
11 cm of caliber　12 cm in height

三彩盖罐

唐代
陶器
二级文物
腹径 12.7 厘米
高 13 厘米

Tri-colored jar with lid
Tang Dynasty
Pottery
Second-class cultural relics
12.7 cm of belly diameter
13 cm in height

三彩罐
唐代
陶器
二级文物
高 19.7 厘米　腹径 22 厘米
口径 12.8 厘米

Tri-colored jar
Tang Dynasty
Pottery
Second-class cultural relics
19.7 cm in height　22 cm of belly diameter
12.8 cm of caliber

三彩罐

唐代

陶器

二级文物

高 23 厘米　口径 10 厘米

底径 9 厘米　腹径 18.3 厘米

Tri–colored jar

Tang Dynasty

Pottery

Second–class cultural relics

23 cm in height　10 cm of caliber

9 cm of base diameter　18.3 cm of belly diameter

00626

三彩三足罐

唐代

陶器

二级文物

高 14.2 厘米　腹径 18 厘米

口径 11.2 厘米

Tri-colored jar with three legs

Tang Dynasty

Pottery

Second-class cultural relics

14.2 cm in height　18 cm of belly diameter

11.2 cm of caliber

三彩宽条纹圈足罐

唐代

陶器

一级文物

高 24.5 厘米　腹径 24 厘米

口径 11 厘米　底径 14 厘米

Tri-colored wide-striped jar with round base

Tang Dynasty

Pottery

First-class cultural relics

24.5 cm in height　24 cm of belly diameter

11 cm of caliber　14 cm of base diameter

三彩宝相花盘

陶器

二级文物

口径17.4厘米

底径7.1厘米　高4.3厘米

Tri-colored tray inlaid with magnolia

Pottery

Second-class cultural relics

17.4 cm of caliber

7.1 cm of base diameter　4.3 cm in height

三彩人形注七星盘

唐代

陶器

二级文物

高 4.2 厘米　口径 24 厘米

Tri-colored tray with smann pieces

Tang Dynasty

Pottery

Second-class cultural relics

4.2 cm in height　24 cm of caliber

三彩九星盘

唐代
陶器
二级文物
口径 24.2 厘米　底径 12.4 厘米
高 4.2 厘米　盂高 6.5 厘米

Tri-colored tray with nine pieces
Tang Dynasty
Pottery
Second-class cultural relics
24.2 cm of caliber　12.4 cm of base diameter
4.2 cm in height　6.5 cm in height of spittoon

三彩飞雁花纹三足盘

唐代

陶器

二级文物

高6.5厘米　口径30厘米

Tri-colored tray with three legs and inlaid with flying goose

Tang Dynasty

Pottery

Second-class cultural relics

6.5 cm in height　30 cm of caliber

三彩九星盘	
唐代	Tri-colored tray with nine pieces
陶器	Tang Dynasty
二级文物	Pottery
	Second-class cultural relics
口径 24.4 厘米	24.4 cm of caliber
通高 4.4 厘米	4.4 cm in height

三彩荷花纹三足盘

唐代
陶器
二级文物
高 6.8 厘米
口径 27.3 厘米

Tri-colored tray with three legs and lotus-flower stripes
Tang Dynasty
Pottery
Second-class cultural relics
6.8 cm in height
27.3 cm of caliber

三彩飞雁荷花三足盘

唐代	Tri-colored tray with three legs and wild-goose-flying stripes
陶器	Tang Dynasty
一级文物	Pottery
口径 28 厘米	First-class cultural relics
高 6.2 厘米	28 cm of caliber
	6.2 cm in height

三彩七星盘

唐代	Tri-colored tray with seven pieces
陶器	Tang Dynasty
二级文物	Pottery
高 3.7 厘米	Second-class cultural relics
口径 24.7 厘米	3.7 cm in height
	24.7 cm of caliber

三彩七星盘

唐代
陶器
二级文物
盘高 4.2 厘米
口径 26.5 厘米

Tri-colored tray with seven pieces
Tang Dynasty
Pottery
Second-class cultural relics
4.2 cm in height
26.5 cm of caliber

三彩七星盘

唐代

陶器

二级文物

盘高 4.3 厘米　口径 26.5 厘米

Tri-colored tray with seven pieces

Tang Dynasty

Pottery

Second-class cultural relics

4.3 cm in height　26.5 cm of caliber

飞雁三足盘

唐代

陶器

二级文物

口径 17.4 厘米

高 4.2 厘米

Tri-colored dish with three legs and decorated with flying goose design

Tang Dynasty

Pottery

Second-class cultural relics

17.4 cm of caliber

4.2 cm of height

三彩七星盘

唐代
陶器
二级文物

Tri-colored tray with seven pieces
Tang Dynasty
Pottery
Second-class cultural relics

三彩鸭衔荷叶杯

唐代	Tri-colored cup shaped in a duck-holding lotus
陶器	Tang Dynasty
二级文物	Pottery
长 12.4 厘米	Second-class cultural relics
高 7 厘米	12.4 cm in length
	7 cm in height

绿釉白斑杯

唐代	Green-glazed cup with white spots
陶器	Tang Dynasty
二级文物	Pottery
	Second-class cultural relics
口径 8.1 厘米	8.1 cm of caliber
底径 4 厘米　高 6 厘米	4 cm of base diameter　6 cm in height

三彩杯

唐代	Tri-colored cup
陶器	Tang Dynasty
二级文物	Pottery
	Second-class cultural relics
高 6.1 厘米	6.1 cm in height
口径 7.8 厘米	7.8 cm of caliber

三彩龙首杯	
陶器	Tri-colored cup shaped in Loong's head
二级文物	Pottery
口径19厘米	Second-class cultural relics
底径13厘米	19 cm of caliber
	13 cm of base diameter

三彩单耳杯
唐代
陶器
二级文物
高 5.6 厘米
口径 4.9 厘米　底径 3.4 厘米

Tri-colored pot with a single handle
Tang Dynasty
Pottery
Second-class cultural relics
5.6 cm in height
4.9 cm of caliber　3.4 cm of base diameter

三彩碗
唐代
陶器
二级文物
口径10.8厘米　高4.7厘米

Tri-colored bowl
Tang Dynasty
Pottery
Second-class cultural relics
10.8 cm of caliber　4.7 cm in height

黄绿釉碗

唐代
陶器
二级文物
高 4.7 厘米
口径 11 厘米　底径 6.7 厘米

Yellow and green glazed bowl
Tang Dynasty
Pottery
Second-class cultural relics
4.7 cm in height
11 cm of caliber　6.7 cm of base diameter

三彩雕花平底碗

唐代	Tri-colored flat-based bowl inlaid with flowers
陶器	Tang Dynasty
二级文物	Pottery
	Second-class cultural relics
口径 10 厘米　高 4 厘米	10 cm of caliber　4 cm in height

三彩小钵
唐代
陶器
二级文物
高3.7厘米　口径9.3厘米

Tri-colored small earthen bowl
Tang Dynasty
Pottery
Second-class cultural relics
3.7 cm in height　9.3 cm of caliber

黄釉执贴花执壶

唐代
陶器
二级文物
口径 6.2 厘米
底径 7.3 厘米　高 14.2 厘米

Yellow-glazed jar inlaid with applique
Tang Dynasty
Pottery
Second-class cultural relics
6.2 cm of caliber
7.3 cm of base diameter　14.2 cm in height

三彩凤首壶

唐代	Tri-colored pot shaped in phoenix head
陶器	Tang Dynasty
二级文物	Pottery
高29.4厘米	Second-class cultural relics
	29.4 cm in height

三彩兽头壶
唐代
陶器
一级文物
高27.5厘米
口径4厘米　底径9.4厘米

Tri-colored pot shaped in beast head
Tang Dynasty
Pottery
First-class cultural relics
27.5 cm in height
4 cm of caliber　9.4 cm of base diameter

三彩人执荷叶注

陶器

二级文物

高 13.3 厘米

Tri-colored lotus-leaf-shaped funnel held by a male figure

Pottery

Second-class cultural relics

13.3 cm in height

绿釉水注

陶器
二级文物
口径 7 厘米
底径 7.3 厘米　高 14 厘米

Green-glazed water funnel
Pottery
Second-class cultural relics
7 cm of caliber
7.3 cm of base diameter　14 cm in height

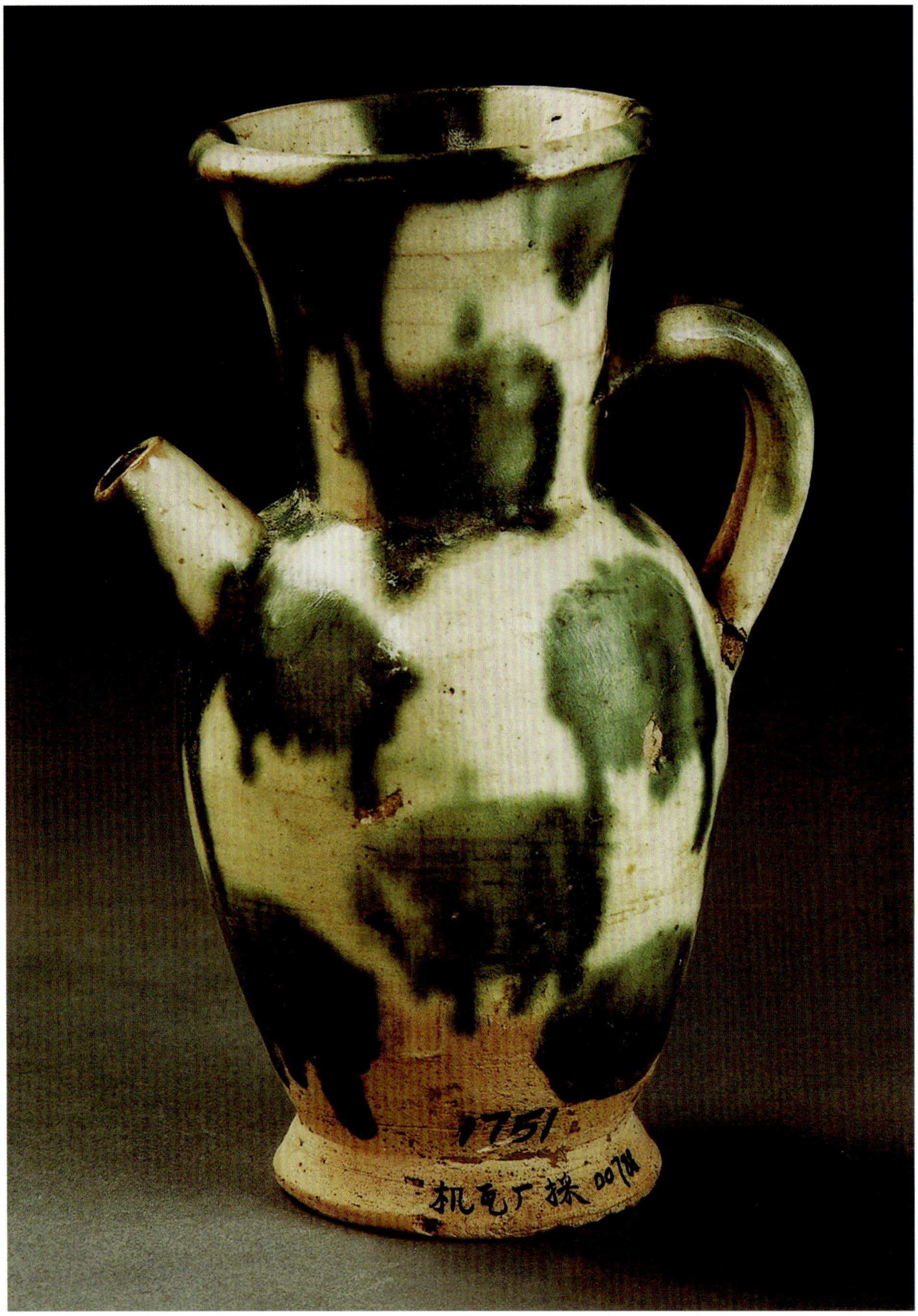

三彩注子
陶器
二级文物
高 16 厘米
口径 7.1 厘米

Tri-colored kettle
Pottery
Second-class cultural relics
16 cm in height
7.1 cm of caliber

三彩高颈瓶

唐代 | Tri-colored bottle with a high neck

陶器 | Tang Dynasty

Pottery

二级文物 | Second-class cultural relics

口径6.7厘米 | 6.7 cm of caliber

底径8厘米　高21.4厘米 | 8 cm of base diameter　21.4 cm in height

三彩豆
陶器
二级文物
口径 19 厘米　底径 13 厘米
高 11.3 厘米

Tri-colored stemmed bowl
Pottery
Second-class cultural relics
19 cm of caliber　13 cm of base diameter
11.3 cm in height

三彩珍珠纹豆

唐代

陶器

二级文物

高 7.2 厘米

口径 11.2 厘米　底径 7.1 厘米

Tri-colored stemmed bowl with pearl stripes

Tang Dynasty

Pottery

Second-class cultural relics

7.2 cm in height

11.2 cm of caliber　7.1 cm of base diameter

38

三彩豆	
唐代	Tri-colored stemmed bowl
陶器	Tang Dynasty
二级文物	Pottery
	Second-class cultural relics
口径13厘米　底径7.2厘米	13 cm of caliber　7.2 cm of base diameter
高6.8厘米	6.8 cm in height

三彩莲花形口乳钉纹盏

唐代
陶器
二级文物
口径 17.7 厘米
底径 9.3 厘米　高 6.9 厘米

Tri-colored lotus-shaped bowl with white strips
Tang Dynasty
Pottery
Second-class cultural relics
17.7 cm of caliber
9.3 cm of base diameter　6.9 cm in height

三彩白斑粉盒

唐代	Tri-colored powder box with spots
陶器	Tang Dynasty
二级文物	Pottery
高 4.3 厘米	Second-class cultural relics
口径 8.4 厘米	4.3 cm in height
	8.4 cm of caliber

三彩粉盒	
唐代	Tri-colored powder box
陶器	Tang Dynasty
二级文物	Pottery
	Second-class cultural relics
高3.8厘米　直径9.2厘米	3.8 cm in height　9.2 cm of diameter

三彩盂
唐代
陶器
二级文物
高 6.2 厘米　口径 3.7 厘米

Tri-colored receptacle
Tang Dynasty
Pottery
Second-class cultural relics
6.2 cm in height　3.7 cm of caliber

三彩脉枕	
陶器	Tri-colored pulse-feeling cushion
二级文物	Pottery
高 4.8 厘米	Second-class cultural relics
	4.6 cm in height
横 8.9 厘米　纵 11.2 厘米	8.9 cm in width　11.2 cm in length

三彩鸳鸯枕

唐代	Tri-colored pillow with mandarin ducks
陶器	Tang Dynasty
	Pottery
一级文物	First-class cultural relics
长 12 厘米　宽 10 厘米	12 cm in length　10 cm in width
厚 5.2 厘米	5.2 cm in thickness

三彩枕	
唐代	Tri-colored pillow
陶器	Tang Dynasty
二级文物	Pottery
长10厘米　宽12.5厘米	Second-class cultural relics
高5厘米	10 cm in length　12.5 cm in width
	5 cm in height

三彩粉盒
陶器
二级文物
直径10厘米
通高3.6厘米

Tri-colored powder box
Pottery
Second-class cultural relics
10 cm of diameter
3.6 cm in height

三彩牛车
唐代
陶器
二级文物
通高26.6厘米　车长23.1厘米
牛长17厘米　牛高12.3厘米

Tri-colored carriage and cow
Tang Dynasty
Pottery
Second-class cultural relics
26.6 cm in general height　23.1 cm in length of cart
17 cm in length of cow　12.3 cm in height of cow

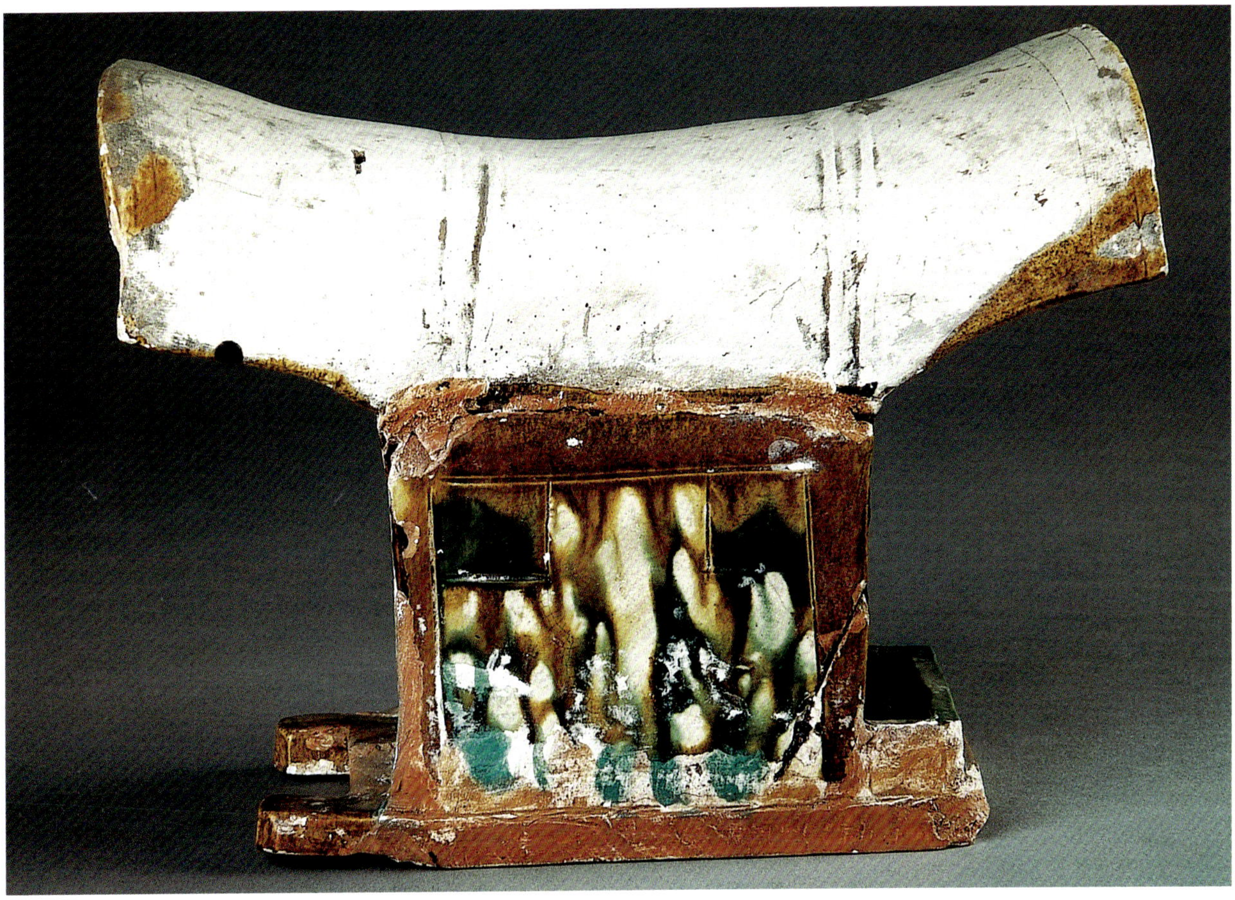

三彩器座

唐代	Tri-colored stand
陶器	Tang Dynasty
二级文物	Pottery
高8厘米	Second-class cultural relics
面径12.9厘米	8 cm in height
底径11.2厘米	12.9 cm of top diameter
	11.2 cm of base diameter

三彩褐釉双龙尊

唐代

陶器

二级文物

高 31.5 厘米　底径 8 厘米

Tri-colored brown-glazed jar with double Loongs

Tang Dynasty

Pottery

Second-class cultural relics

31.5 cm in height　8 cm of base diameter

三彩黄釉双龙尊

唐代

陶器

二级文物

高35厘米

口径10厘米　底径10厘米

Tri-colored yellow-glazed jar with double Loongs

Tang Dynasty

Pottery

Second-class cultural relics

35cm in height

10 cm of caliber　10 cm of base diameter

三彩环底人足炉

唐代

陶器

一级文物

高 8.6 厘米　口径 12.5 厘米

Tri-colored stove with a round base

Tang Dynasty

Pottery

First-class cultural relics

8.6 cm in height　12.5 cm of caliber

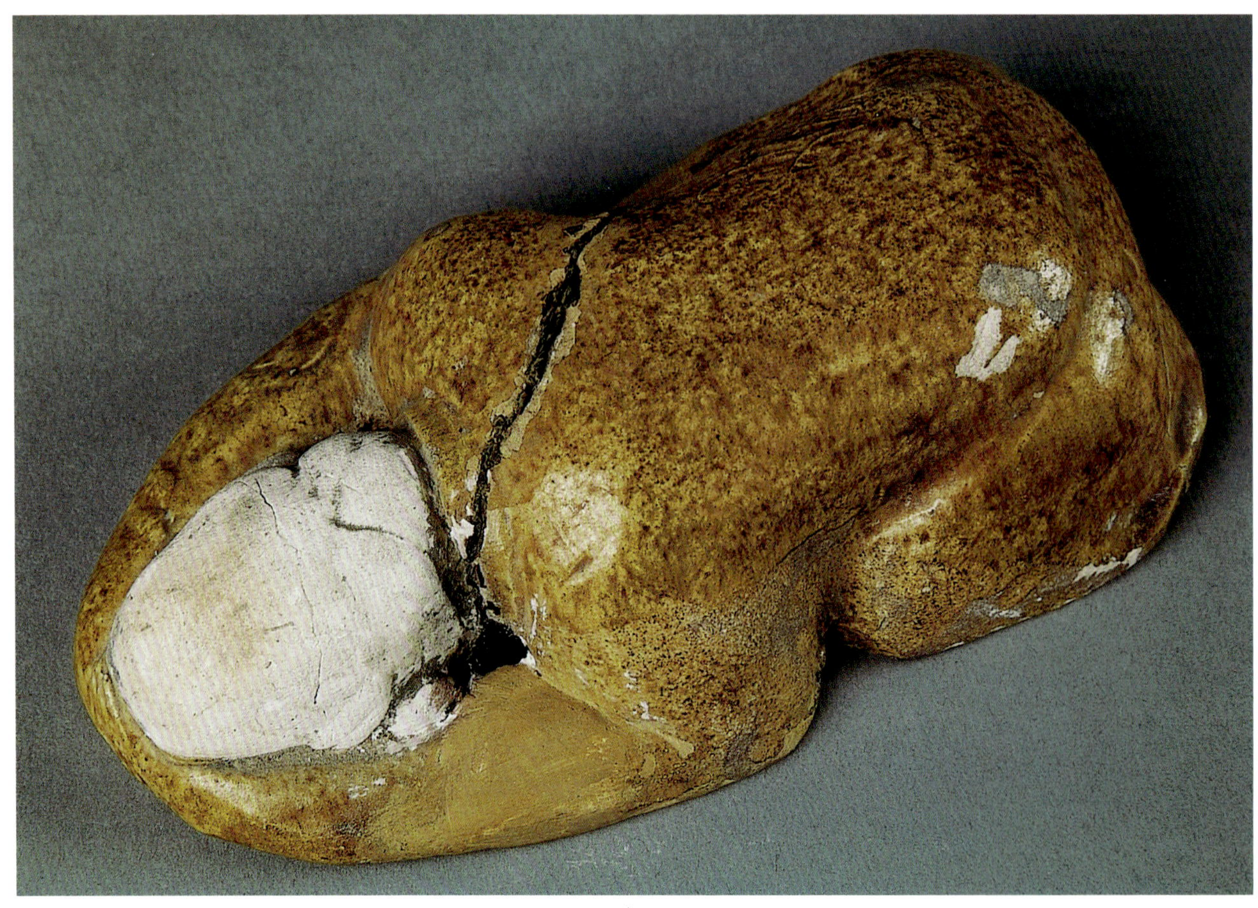

三彩黄釉匍匐俑

唐代	Tri-colored yellow-glazed grape-crawling figure
陶器	Tang Dynasty
二级文物	Pottery
	Second-class cultural relics
长 13.7 厘米	13.7 cm in length
宽 7.7 厘米　高 3.9 厘米	7.7 cm in width　3.9 cm in height